Walt Disney's
Treasury of
Children's Classics

WALT DISNEY'S

TREASURY OF CHIL
CLA

EDITED BY

HARRY N. ABRAMS, INC.,

DREN'S
SSICS

Illustrated with original animation art and stills from the great Disney films

Darlene Geis

Publishers, NEW YORK

Copy Editor: Margaret Donovan
Designer: Dirk Luykx
Library of Congress Catalog Card Number: 78-3529

Published by The Reader's Digest Association, Inc., 1991, by permission of Harry N. Abrams, Incorporated, New York.

Library of Congress Cataloging in Publication Data
Main entry under title:
Walt Disney's treasury of children's classics.
SUMMARY: Retells seventeen well-known fairy tales, folk tales, and short stories illustrated with scenes from Walt Disney films. Includes a behind-the-scenes look at the production of animated films.
1. Children's stories, American. 2. Children's stories, English. 3. Fairy tales. 4. Tales. 5. Animation (Cinematography)—Juvenile literature. [1. Short stories. 2. Fairy tales. 3. Folklore. 4. Animation (Cinematography) I. Geis, Darlene. II. Title: Treasury of children's classics.
PZ5. W167 [Fic] 78-3529
ISBN 0-8109-0812-3

Dedicated to Walt Disney
whose artistry and imagination
animated the favorite stories of our childhood,
brought to life the beloved characters,
and enabled us to step, enchanted,
into the world of fantasy

CONTENTS

Fairy Tales

Classics

Contemporary Stories

Fairy Tales

Cinde

From Walt Disney's Motion Picture *Cinderella*,
based on the original classic by Charles Perrault

Once upon a time in a faraway land, a widowed gentleman lived in a fine house with his only daughter. He gave his beloved child everything her heart desired—beautiful dresses, a horse, a puppy. Still, he felt she needed a mother's care. So he married again, choosing a woman with two young daughters who, he hoped, would be playmates for his little girl.

Sad to say, the good man died a short time later, and the stepmother then began to show her true nature. She was harsh and cold, and bitterly jealous of her stepdaughter's sweetness and beauty, qualities that made her own daughters, Anastasia and Drizella, seem even meaner and uglier by contrast.

The stepsisters were richly dressed, but the poor girl was forced to wear a coarse, plain dress and apron and do all the hardest jobs in the house. She got up before daybreak, carried water, lit the fires, cooked

and washed and scrubbed. When she had done her work, she used to go to the chimney-corner and sit down there among the cinders and ashes to keep warm. Thus she came to be called Cinderella.

Her stepmother and sisters slept in beautiful chambers, but Cinderella's tiny bedroom was up in the garret under the roof of the house, where dozens of mice lived. And yet, through it all, Cinderella remained gentle and kind, dreaming that someday happiness would come to her.

She made friends with the birds who woke her each morning. She made friends with the mice who shared her garret. She gave names to all the mice, and sewed them tiny coats and hats. For their part, the mice loved Cinderella and were grateful to her because she sometimes rescued them from a trap or saved them from Lucifer, her stepmother's bad-tempered cat.

Each morning Cinderella made breakfast for the household: a bowl of milk for the cat, a bone for the dog, oats for her old horse, corn and grain for the chickens, geese, and ducks in the barnyard. Then she carried breakfast trays upstairs for her stepmother and Anastasia and Drizella.

"Take that ironing and have it back in an hour," Drizella demanded.

"Don't forget the mending and don't be all day getting it done," Anastasia scolded.

"Pick up the laundry and get on with your duties," her stepmother ordered. "Scrub the large carpet in the main hall, wash the windows, clean the tapestries."

"Yes, Drizella. Yes, Anastasia. Yes, Stepmother," Cinderella replied, as she set about her tasks cheerfully enough.

Now it happened that on the other side of town in the Royal Palace the

King and the Grand Duke were talking. "It's high time the Prince married and settled down!" said the old King.

"But, Your Majesty," replied the Duke, "first he must meet a girl and fall in love."

"You're right," the King agreed. "We'll give a ball and invite every young girl in my kingdom. He's bound to fall in love with one of them."

When the invitations to the ball were delivered, Anastasia and Drizella danced for joy. "A ball! A ball! We're going to a ball!" they exclaimed.

"I am invited, too," said Cinderella. "It says, 'By royal command, every eligible maiden is to attend.' "

The stepsisters laughed at the idea of Cinderella going to a ball wearing her apron and carrying a broom. But her stepmother, with a sly smile, said of course Cinderella could go—*if* she finished her work and *if* she had a suitable dress to wear.

"IF," laughed Anastasia.

"IF," Drizella giggled.

All day long the stepsisters were busy choosing gowns, petticoats, and ornaments to wear in their hair. All day long they talked of nothing but how they should be dressed for the ball. Meanwhile Cinderella was kept busier than ever, for it was she who had to iron the full skirts, pleat the ruffles, and tie the ribbons into bows.

When the carriage came to take the stepmother and her two

daughters to the ball, Cinderella had not had a minute to get herself ready. "Well," said her stepmother, "then you're not going. Oh, what a shame! But there will be other times and other balls." And she and her ugly daughters swept out to the coach.

Cinderella climbed the dark stairs to her room and gazed sadly out of the moonlit window at the distant castle. Suddenly, a light appeared behind her. Turning, she saw that her candle had been lit and in its glow hung a lovely party dress. Her friends the birds and the mice had made it for her as a surprise, trimming it with bits of ribbon and beads they had found about the house.

In no time at all Cinderella slipped into the dress, thanked her friends, and ran down the stairs, calling, "Please wait, I'm coming, too!" But when Anastasia and Drizella saw her they were furious. "My beads!" screamed one. "My ribbon!" howled the other. "You're a little thief!" And they snatched at Cinderella's dress until it was torn to rags.

In tears, Cinderella ran across the yard to the garden. There she flung herself on a bench and sobbed, "It's just no use. Nothing will help. I give up." But at that moment, out of a cloud of magic stardust, appeared a round-faced little woman in a hooded cloak, "Nonsense,

child," she said in a sweet voice. "Dry those tears—you can't go to the ball looking like that."

Cinderella stopped crying and asked, "Who are you?"

"I'm your fairy godmother," said the woman, "and we don't have much time. I think the first thing you'll need is a pumpkin." Cinderella couldn't guess why, but she obediently fetched a large pumpkin. The godmother waved her wand over it and sang the magic words, "Salaga-doola, menchicka boola, bibbidi-bobbidi-boo." The pumpkin slowly rose on its vine, while its tendrils curled into wheels. In no time it had become a handsome coach.

"Now," said the godmother, "we'll need some mice." Four of Cinderella's little friends scurried forward, and once again the god-mother sang the magic words as she touched the mice with her wand. Four dapple-gray horses appeared and were hitched to the coach.

Then the godmother changed Cinderella's old horse into a proud coachman, and Bruno the dog into an elegant footman. "And now for you, my dear," said the fairy godmother, tapping Cinderella with her wand. Instantly the torn dress became a lovely silken gown. Peeping out from under its skirt were dainty glass slippers, the prettiest in the whole world.

As Cinderella got into the coach, her godmother commanded her, above all things, not to stay at the ball past twelve o'clock. For if she stayed one minute longer than midnight, the coach would become a pumpkin again, her horses mice, her coachman an old horse, and her footman a dog, while she herself would be dressed in rags. Cinderella promised to leave the ball before midnight, and she set off joyfully for the Royal Palace.

The ball had already started when she arrived, and the Prince was politely bowing to the two-hundred-tenth and -eleventh young ladies—Anastasia and Drizella. Suddenly, the Prince looked up and saw in the doorway of the palace the most beautiful girl he had ever beheld. Entranced, he walked past the sisters toward Cinderella, took her hand, and led her into the great hall among all the company.

The King's son wouldn't dance with anyone else the rest of the evening, and not for a minute would he let go of Cinderella's hand. Her

sisters and her stepmother, never recognizing Cinderella, wondered who the beautiful stranger might be. All the ladies studied her clothes and headdress and vowed to copy them the very next day. But the old King chuckled contentedly because his plan had worked—the Prince had indeed found the bride of his dreams.

When the palace clock began to strike midnight, Cinderella remembered her promise. "I must go," she cried in a panic, and, freeing her hand from the Prince's, she ran through the palace and down a flight of stairs, with the Prince and the Duke in pursuit. One of her tiny glass slippers fell off, but she ran on and leapt into her waiting coach.

The clock was still striking as the coach sped away from the palace. As it passed through the gates, the clock struck twelve. Coach, horses, and all vanished, and in their place was a pumpkin, some mice, a dog, an old horse, and Cinderella in her ragged dress. All that remained of the magical evening was one glass slipper sparkling on her foot.

The next morning the King's son had it proclaimed throughout the land that he would marry the girl who had lost her slipper at the ball the night before. He sent the Grand Duke to travel about the kingdom in search of the girl whose foot would exactly fit the glass slipper. The Duke tried the little slipper on every princess, every duchess, and all the Court, but in vain. Finally he came to Cinderella's house.

The stepmother, in great excitement, went to rouse her lazy daughters. "We haven't a moment to lose," she cried. "There is a chance that one of you can become the Prince's bride if the glass slipper fits you!" And she sent them scurrying down to the Duke with the warning, "Don't fail me."

Then she followed Cinderella, who had gone to her room to make herself presentable for the Duke, and locked her in. No one else was to have a chance at so great a prize.

When Cinderella heard the click of the lock she realized, too late, what had happened. "Please, oh please, you must let me out!" she called, rattling the doorknob. But her stepmother dropped the key in her pocket and walked away, laughing her meanest laugh. She did not

know that two little mice followed her down the stairs, never taking their eyes off the pocket where the key rested.

Meanwhile Drizella and Anastasia were arguing over the glass slipper, each claiming it as her own. The stepmother watched as first Anastasia and then Drizella tried to squeeze a large foot into the tiny slipper, without success. She did not notice that two quiet mice were busily stealing the key to Cinderella's door from her pocket and carrying it away.

The Grand Duke took the slipper from the unhappy stepsisters and prepared to be off with it to the next house, when Cinderella called from the stairs, "Please wait, Your Grace. May I try the slipper?" The

stepmother tried to block her path. "It's only Cinderella, our scullery maid," she told the Duke, but he brushed her aside. "Madam, my orders were 'every maiden in the land.'"

The wicked stepmother had one more trick left. She tripped the Duke's servant, who was carrying the glass slipper, and it fell to the floor, where it shattered into hundreds of pieces. "Oh! this is terrible!" cried the Duke. "What will the King say?"

Cinderella reached into a pocket under her apron. "See," she said, "I have the other slipper." The Duke slipped it on her foot, which, of course, it fit perfectly. Thereupon the fairy godmother appeared, and touched Cinderella with her wand, and all could see that she was indeed the unknown beauty who had captured the Prince's heart at the ball.

Cinderella was driven to the Royal Palace in the King's own coach. There, amid great rejoicing and the ringing of all the bells in the kingdom, Cinderella married her Prince.

AND THEY LIVED HAPPILY EVER AFTER.

CINDERELLA

The Story of the Production

One of the great Disney animation classics, *Cinderella* is based on the rags-to-riches fairy tale written by Charles Perrault nearly three hundred years ago. The Disney Studio spent $2.5 million and six years —from 1944 to 1950—on the production, experimenting with new techniques, modeling on the characters to give them roundness, and embellishing the artwork with extravagant detail.

Cinderella's musical score has six songs, each woven into the picture and making an important point in the story: "Cinderella," "So This Is Love," "A Dream Is a Wish Your Heart Makes," "Cinderella's Work Song," "Bibbidi-Bobbidi-Boo (The Magic Song)," and "Sing, Sweet Nightingale."

Besides a cast of nine actors and actresses who were responsible for the voice characterizations, a staff of more than sixty animators, artists, writers, directors, musical directors, and editors were involved in the production—all under the exacting supervision of Walt Disney himself. Since its premiere in 1950, the picture has been released every seven or eight years and has played in a dozen languages to audiences on all seven continents.

The multiplane camera can shoot several layers of animation painted on glass against an opaque background, thus producing a marvelous illusion of depth. Here a crew of ten technicians operates the complex machine; the man at the upper left is Card Walker who, many years later, became Chairman and Chief Executive Officer of Walt Disney Productions

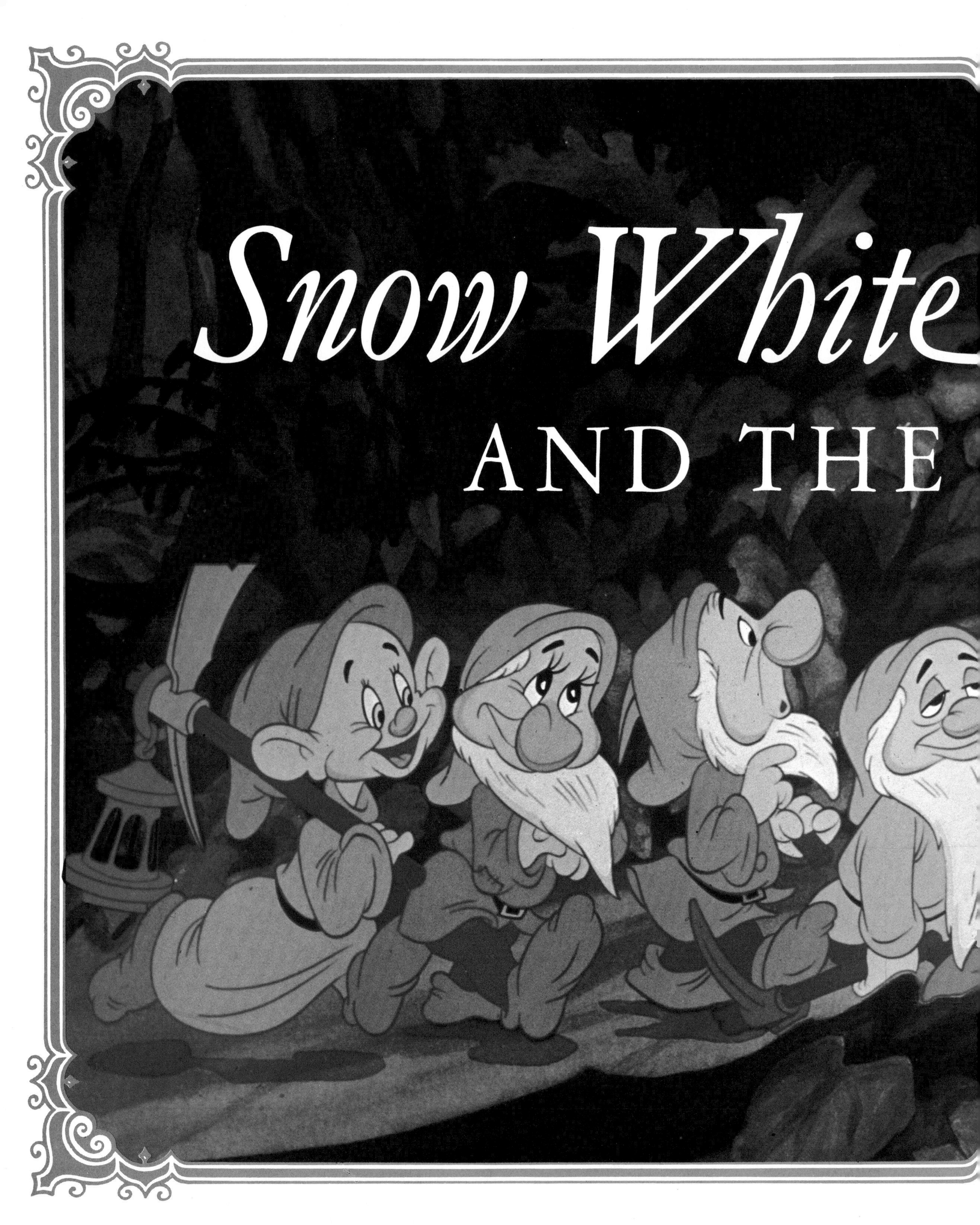

Snow White AND THE

SEVEN DWARFS

From Walt Disney's Motion Picture *Snow White and the Seven Dwarfs,* adapted from Grimms' Fairy Tales

nce in midwinter when the snowflakes were falling from the sky like feathers, a Queen sat sewing at a window with an ebony frame. As she was sewing and looking out at the snowflakes, she pricked her finger with her needle and three drops of blood fell on the snow. The red looked so beautiful on the white snow that she thought to herself: "If only I had a child as white as snow and as red as blood and as black as the wood of my window frame." Some time later she gave birth to a daughter who was as white as snow and as red as blood, and her hair was as black as ebony. They called her Snow White, and when she was born the Queen died.

A year later the lonely King took a second wife. She was beautiful, but she was cruel and jealous and couldn't bear the thought that anyone might be more beautiful than she. She had a magic mirror and every day when she looked into it she asked:

Mirror, mirror on the wall,
Who is the fairest of us all?

and the mirror answered:

You, O Queen, are the fairest in the land.

That set her mind at rest, for she knew the mirror told the truth.

But as Snow White grew, she became more and more beautiful, and the Queen feared that someday the girl would be the fairest in the land. So she dressed Snow White in rags and forced her to live with the servants and to slave from sunrise to sundown.

All the while that Snow White cheerfully scrubbed floors and dusted and carried water from the well, she dreamed that her Prince Charming would come and carry her off to his castle in the clouds. One day, as she was drawing water from the well, her friends the pigeons told her a secret. It was really a wishing well! "Make a wish into the well," they said, "and if you hear it echo, your wish will come true."

Snow White spoke into the well, "I'm wishing for the one I love to find me today."

Before the echo could repeat the whole wish, a handsome Prince on horseback rode up and saw Snow White. He looked at her with such admiration that Snow White grew embarrassed and ran off to her room. But the jealous Queen had been watching from her window, and she turned yellow and green with envy.

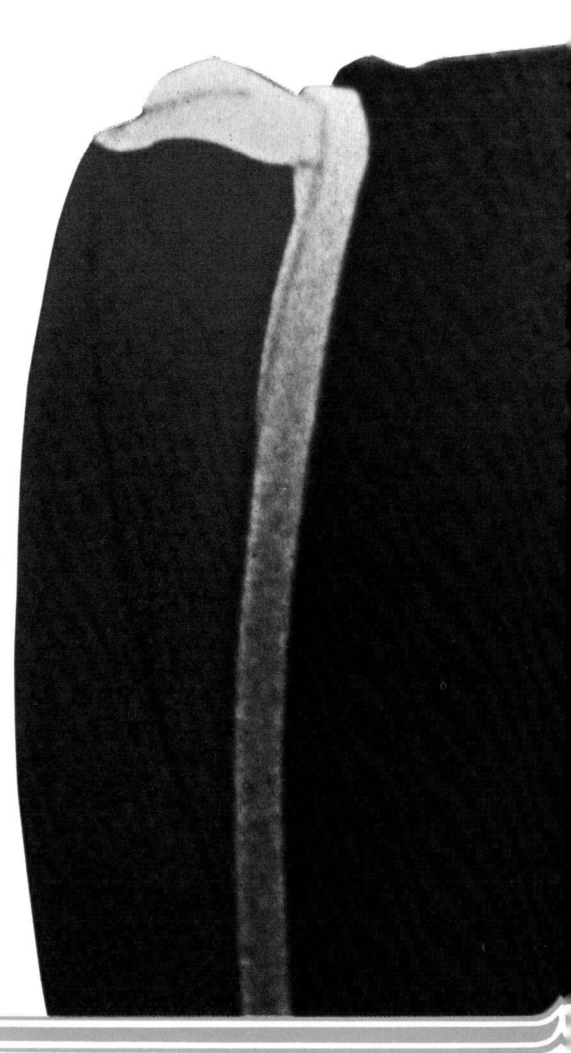

Looking into her mirror she demanded:

Mirror, mirror on the wall,
Who is the fairest of us all?

and this time the mirror replied:

Her lips blood red, her hair like night,
Her skin like snow, her name—
Snow White!

The Queen was in a terrible temper and she sent for her huntsman.

"Get that child out of my sight," she stormed. "Take her far into the forest, kill her, and bring me back her heart in this box, to prove you have done it."

The huntsman was saddened at these words but he did not dare to disobey his Queen. He took Snow White deep into the forest, and as he watched her happily picking wild flowers he knew he could not hurt this lovely girl.

Kneeling before Snow White he said, "I cannot kill you as the Queen commanded. Run away and hide, but do not come back to the palace because the wicked Queen will surely harm you."

The huntsman left Snow White then, and on his way home he killed a young boar and put its heart in the box for the Queen, as proof that he had carried out her orders.

Alone in the great forest, Snow White was frightened by everything she saw, every strange sound she heard. She ran and ran until just before nightfall she saw a tiny cottage, not much larger than a doll's house. No one was at home, so she opened the little door and went in. There were seven dusty little chairs, and seven dirty little dishes, seven little shirts that needed washing, and dirt and cobwebs everywhere.

"From the look of this place, it belongs to seven untidy little children," Snow White said, and she went about sweeping and cleaning and scrubbing and laundering—all with the help of some friendly woodland creatures who had followed her. They sang and danced and whistled while they worked, and in no time at all the little house was spotless.

Then Snow White went upstairs and there she found seven little

beds, each with a name carved on it: "DOC, HAPPY, SNEEZY, DOPEY, GRUMPY, BASHFUL, SLEEPY." "What funny names for children!" said Snow White and she yawned, "I'm a little sleepy myself." And flopping down across the beds, she fell sound asleep.

When it was quite dark the owners of the little house came home. They were seven dwarfs who went off to the mountains every day with their picks and shovels to mine diamonds. They no sooner had lighted their seven candles than they saw that someone had been in their house. "The whole place is clean!" Doc exclaimed. "There's dirty work afoot," growled Grumpy.

Cautiously they tiptoed up the stairs, and there they found Snow White, asleep on their beds. "What is it?" Bashful and Happy asked. "Why," said Doc, "I think it's a girl!" "She's mighty purty," Sneezy said. Bashful sighed, "She's beautiful. Like an angel." At that Snow White woke up.

When she saw the seven dwarfs she was startled. "Why you're not children at all. You're little men," she exclaimed. But they were friendly, and asked her name and how she came to their house.

Snow White told them how her stepmother had tried to have her killed and that the huntsman had spared her life. "The Queen will never find me here and if you let me stay, I'll keep house for you and do the cooking, make the beds, wash, and sew," she promised. The dwarfs whispered together and then they said, "If you keep everything neat and clean you can stay with us and you'll want for nothing."

So Snow White stayed and kept the house in order. In the mornings the dwarfs went off to look for diamonds, and in the evenings when they came home, dinner was ready. Snow White was alone all day and the kindly dwarfs warned her, "Watch out for your Stepmother. She's full of black magic and she knows everything. Don't let anyone in while we're away."

In the meantime, the Queen had been given the box with the heart, which she believed was Snow White's. She felt sure she was again the most beautiful of all. One day she went to her mirror and asked:

> Magic mirror on the wall,
> Who now is the fairest one of all?

But the truthful mirror answered:

> Over the seven jewelled hills,
> Beyond the seventh fall,
> In the cottage of the seven dwarfs
> Dwells Snow White, fairest one of all.

Then the Queen stamped her foot in a fury. The huntsman had tricked her, and Snow White still lived. As long as the girl lived, the Queen could not be the fairest one of all, and she *had* to be or jealousy would leave her no peace. At last she thought up a plan. She stained her face and hands and dressed in black rags like a toothless old peddler woman. No one would ever recognize her. She went to a secret room that no one else knew about and there she made a poisoned apple. It was beautiful, juicy-looking, shiny red, and anyone who saw it would want a bite. But one taste and the person's eyes would close forever in the Sleeping Death.

Pleased with herself, the Queen made her way to the little cottage in the forest. Hiding behind a tree she watched the seven dwarfs say good-bye to Snow White. "Don't let anybody in the house," they warned her. Then they marched off to their mountain, singing "Heigh-ho, heigh-ho, it's off to work we go. . . ."

No sooner were the dwarfs out of sight than the ragged old woman went to the window and asked Snow White for a drink of water. "Thank you, my pet," she said, when the girl handed it to her through the

window. "Now here's an apple for you," and she cackled wickedly. "Wait till you taste it, dearie, it's delicious!" Snow White reached for the poisoned apple, though her friends, the woodland creatures, tried to keep it from her. No sooner had she taken a bite than she fell to the floor, as if dead.

The birds and animals hurried through the forest to fetch the dwarfs, while the Queen laughed. "Now I'll be the fairest in the land," she said as she slipped away into the forest.

The dwarfs dashed up to the cottage too late to save Snow White.

But they saw the wicked Queen running into the woods, and they ran after her as fast as their little legs would carry them. They chased her to the top of a high cliff, and there the Queen tripped and plunged over the edge. With a terrible scream, she vanished forever.

Sadly the dwarfs returned home. Heartbroken, they looked at their beautiful Snow White, her cheeks and lips still red, as if she were asleep. The dwarfs made a crystal coffin for Snow White and set it in a glade in the forest. Night and day they kept watch over it.

A long time passed, and one day Prince Charming heard about the beautiful Princess asleep in the forest. He wondered if it was the girl he had lost his heart to long ago near the wishing well, and whom he had been seeking ever since. He rode deep into the woods and there he found her, the Princess he loved truly. Leaning over, he kissed her lips. Snow White opened her eyes as if awakening from a deep sleep; the spell of the poisoned apple had been broken by Love's First Kiss.

And Snow White's dearest wish came true. Her Prince rode off with her to his Castle in the Clouds, amid the cheers and good wishes of the dwarfs and forest creatures.

SNOW WHITE AND THE SEVEN DWARFS

The Story of the Production

Walt Disney's first attempt at making a feature-length cartoon was *Snow White and the Seven Dwarfs,* a milestone in motion picture history. Based on a fairy tale by the Brothers Grimm, Disney's eighty-three-minute entertainment is one of the most popular and beloved movies ever made. Once known as Disney's Folly, it is now called Disney's Masterpiece.

"You should have heard the howls of warning when we started making a full-length cartoon," Walt Disney recalled years later. "But there was only one way we could do it successfully and that was to plunge ahead and go for broke—shoot the works. There could be no compromising on money, talent, or time. Well, as everyone knows, the picture did make money, and if it hadn't, there wouldn't be any Disney Studio today."

Production began in 1934 and was completed in 1937. More than 750 artists worked on the picture, creating at least one million drawings, of which over 250,000 were used. Studio chemists in the Disney paint laboratories ground their own pigments from special formulas and mixed 1,500 colors and shades for the characters and backgrounds. The multiplane camera, invented and developed by Walt Disney Studio

Walt Disney accepts a special Academy Award from Shirley Temple in 1939—one large and seven dwarf-sized Oscars for *Snow White*

Adriana Caselotti,
the voice of Snow White

technicians, first reached a high degree of perfection in *Snow White and the Seven Dwarfs.* With it, animated scenes achieved a three-dimensional quality because characters and backgrounds could be photographed on several levels or planes.

The Academy of Motion Picture Arts and Sciences gave *Snow White* a special award in 1939, with nine-year-old Shirley Temple making the presentation to Walt Disney of a large golden Oscar and seven miniature replicas. There are eight songs in the picture, several of which are now considered "standards" in the trade: "I'm Wishing," "One Song," "With a Smile and a Song," "Whistle While You Work," "Heigh-Ho," "Bluddle-Uddle-Um-Dum," "The Dwarfs' Yodel Song," and "Some Day My Prince Will Come." The songs have been translated into thirteen languages and are well known throughout the world, wherever this record-breaking picture has played.

Sleeping Beauty

From Walt Disney's Motion Picture *Sleeping Beauty*,
from the story by Charles Perrault

In a faraway land, long ago, lived King Stefan and his fair Queen. For many years they had longed for a child and finally their wish was granted. A daughter was born and they called her Aurora, after the goddess of the dawn, for she filled their lives with sunshine.

To celebrate her birth, a great holiday was proclaimed throughout the kingdom. Knights and ladies, townspeople and peasants, all dressed in their finest clothes and bringing gifts, came to the palace at the King's invitation to see the new baby and wish her well.

King Hubert, who ruled the neighboring country, arrived with his young son, Prince Phillip. The two kings had long dreamed of uniting their lands by the marriage of their children, and on this occasion they announced the betrothal of the infant Princess Aurora to Prince Phillip.

Suddenly, gliding down a shaft of sunlight that slanted into the Great Hall, the tiny figures of three good fairies appeared. Waving their magic wands they floated over to examine the display of the baby's presents. Then they approached the cradle to bestow their gifts on Princess Aurora. "Little Princess, my gift shall be the gift of beauty," said Flora as her wand showered sparkles of fairy dust. "Tiny Princess, my gift shall be the gift of song," said Fauna.

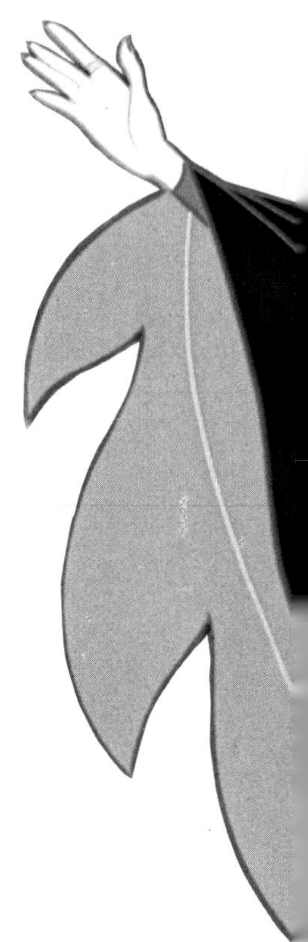

But just as the third fairy, Merryweather, was about to bless the infant with her gift of happiness, a wind blew the castle doors open. There was a blinding flash of lightning, and Maleficent, the evil witch, stood in the center of the hall, furious at not being invited to the festivities. Raising her arms she announced, "I too shall bestow a gift on the child. The Princess shall indeed grow in grace and beauty, beloved by all who know her. But before the sun sets on her sixteenth birthday, she will prick her finger on the spindle of a spinning wheel and—die!"

The poor Queen lifted her baby from the cradle and held her close as if to protect her from the witch's terrible words. The guards encircled Maleficent and lunged at her with their spears, but with her powerful magic she surrounded herself with flames and vanished in a puff of smoke.

Merryweather, who still had her gift to give, quickly waved her wand above the baby saying, "Do not despair, O King and Queen. Though I have not the power to undo this fearful curse, I can help." Then, as her wand created magic pictures in the air, she chanted,

Sweet Princess, if through
This wicked witch's trick
A spindle should your finger prick,
A ray of hope there still may be

In this gift I give to thee.
Not in death but just in sleep
This fateful prophecy you'll keep
And from this slumber you shall wake
When true love's kiss the spell shall break.

King Stefan, still fearful for his daughter's life, decreed that every spinning wheel and spindle in the kingdom should on that very day be burned. A huge bonfire was built in the courtyard and every spinning wheel was destroyed.

The three fairies were not sure that that was enough to keep the Princess safe from harm. They persuaded the King and Queen to let them hide the baby Princess. They would take her to live deep in the forest, all of them disguised as peasants.

And so for sixteen long years the Princess, called Briar Rose by the three good fairies, grew up with them, hidden away in a woodcutter's cottage, with birds and forest creatures for her friends.

Maleficent tried in vain to find the girl, but the good fairies kept her whereabouts well concealed. All these years they lived as mortals, never using their magic for fear that if they did, Maleficent would be able to trace them by its telltale glow.

But on the Princess's sixteenth birthday, Flora, Fauna and Merryweather wanted to surprise her with a cake and a new dress. They sent her out to pick berries in the woods and then they set to work baking a cake and sewing a dress. The cake was a disaster, the dress was awful. "I'm going to get our magic wands," Merryweather declared. "You know, I think she's right," Fauna agreed. It was the only way they had ever made anything.

The wands sent their rays of colored magic shooting around the room, and soon turned the cake into a pastry cook's masterpiece, the dress into a beautiful gown. Unfortunately, the colored sparkles from

their magic drifted up the chimney and out into the sky above the cottage. There Maleficent's raven, who had been hunting for the Princess, saw the magic traces and flew back to his mistress to report that he had found the fairies' hiding place at last.

Meanwhile, Prince Phillip, who happened to be riding through the forest, heard a sweet song. Searching for the singer he found Briar Rose dancing with the woodland creatures and he joined them. As they sang together he and the girl fell in love on the instant. But it was growing late and Briar Rose had to leave.

"When will I see you again?" the eager Prince asked her. "Come to the cottage in the glen this evening," the girl said. "I will be there with my three guardians." And she hurried home to tell Flora, Fauna and Merryweather the wonderful news.

The fairies had news of their own for the girl. "You are really the Princess Aurora, my dear," began Flora. "And tonight we're taking you back to your father, King Stefan." Sadly Briar Rose allowed herself to be led away from the cottage before Prince Phillip came for their meeting. The fairies brought her to her room in the castle where she threw herself

on the bed, sobbing. "Let her have a few moments alone," said Flora, as they closed the door behind them. "Poor dear."

King Stefan and King Hubert had been celebrating the return of the Princess and toasting the future union of their children and their kingdoms. At that moment the arrival of Přince Phillip interrupted their revelries.

"Father," he announced excitedly, "I have just met the girl I am going to marry. Not Princess Aurora, but a peasant girl."

On hearing this, King Hubert raged at his son. When that did no good he pleaded and cajoled, all to no avail. Prince Phillip insisted he would marry the girl he loved. And he galloped off to meet Briar Rose at her cottage in the woods, leaving his father in despair.

All this time Princess Aurora had been weeping alone in her room. There Maleficent, disguised as a wisp of smoke, cast a spell on the girl and led her to a secret room in which there was a magic spinning wheel—the only one left in the entire land. "What can this be?" Aurora wondered. And then she heard a voice commanding, "Touch the spindle!" Her hand reached out to the spindle, it pricked her finger, and at once the Princess fell to the floor in a swoon.

When the three fairies found her stretched out on the stone floor they berated themselves for having left the Princess unguarded even for a minute. They carried her to the finest apartment in the palace and laid her on a bed all embroidered with gold and silver. The Princess was as beautiful as a little angel, her cheeks still rosy, her lips coral. And indeed, although her eyes were shut, she breathed very softly; so they knew she was not dead.

"Come," said Flora, "we'll put everyone in the castle to sleep until the Princess awakens!" The fairies sprinkled sleep-dust on King Stefan,

his Queen, King Hubert, the soldiers and guards, the flag-carriers, the servants—even on the fountains in the courtyard and the candles in the banquet hall. Then they flew off to find Prince Phillip, for only he could awaken the Princess.

When Phillip arrived at the cottage in the forest, Maleficent's henchmen were awaiting him. They chained him and locked him in the witch's dungeon, where he was taunted by Maleficent. She showed him a picture of his peasant girl, Briar Rose, asleep in the tower of King Stefan's castle, and told him she was the Princess Aurora, doomed to sleep until his kiss awakened her. Then, laughing cruelly, Maleficent left the Prince tugging at his chains, locked in the dungeon. It was there the three fairies found him and released him. Arming the Prince with the mighty Sword of Truth and the enchanted Shield of Virtue, they helped him escape from Maleficent's castle.

When Phillip reached the castle of King Stefan, he found the walls overgrown with a forest of thorns while a fire-spouting dragon—

Maleficent in disguise—guarded the drawbridge. The fairies sprinkled magic dust on the Prince's sword, chanting,

> Now, Sword of Truth, fly swift and sure
> That evil die and good endure.

At which the sword flew straight to the dragon's heart, slaying the beast, who turned back into Maleficent as it died.

The Prince ran up the steps of the tower, two at a time, past all the sleeping courtiers, until he reached the chamber where Princess Aurora—his beloved Briar Rose—lay. Gently he kissed her. The Princess awakened, smiled at Phillip, and the whole room lit up. The fountains in the courtyard started to play again, candles flamed once more, the court awoke, and trumpets sounded from the balcony as the Prince and Princess walked down the Grand Stairway hand in hand.

Then before the delighted eyes of King Stefan, the Queen and King Hubert, Phillip and Aurora began to dance to the strains of a romantic waltz. Watching from the musicians' balcony, Fauna started to cry.

"Why Fauna," Flora exclaimed, "Whatever is the matter now?"

Fauna, sobbing, said, "Oh, I just love happy endings!"

And indeed Phillip and Aurora lived happily forever after.

SLEEPING BEAUTY

The Story of the Production

The third, and most ambitious, of Walt Disney's fairy-tale presentations, *Sleeping Beauty* was six years in the making at a cost of $6 million. It was released in 1959.

This animated feature was far more challenging than its predecessors because of the new large Technirama 70mm projection process it employed. Walt Disney explained that the wide screen "imposed added labors on the artists [300 in all]. They had to move their characters in larger fields of action. Every phase of artistry and mechanics, which together comprise the art of animation, had to be revamped."

The richly colored backgrounds were modeled after Renaissance paintings, and as for the characters in Charles Perrault's seventeenth-century classic, Disney instructed his animators to "make them as real as possible, near flesh-and-blood, and sympathetic." One million drawings later, Disney himself called the perfected process "the art of painting in lifelike motion."

The fidelity of the sound, too, was improved to do full justice to Tchaikovsky's lilting *Sleeping Beauty* ballet music that serves as the picture's score. Five songs—"Once Upon a Dream," "I Wonder," "Hail the Princess Aurora," "The Skump Song," and "Sleeping Beauty Song"—contribute to the charm of one of Disney's best-loved films.

The color laboratory in the Studio's ink and paint department prepares the special colors for each production, selecting the pigments and making certain that the paint batches remain consistent

Classics

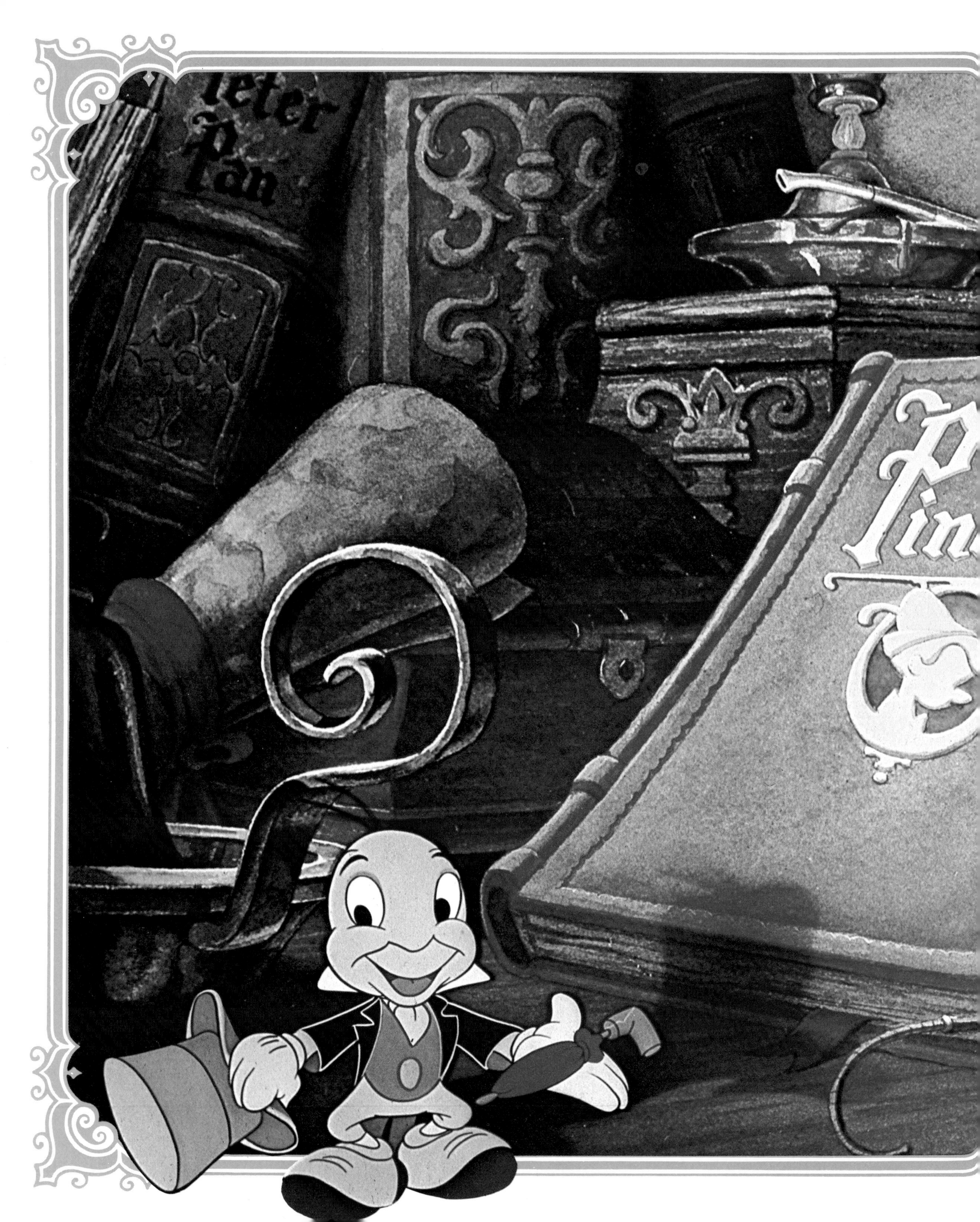
Peter Pan

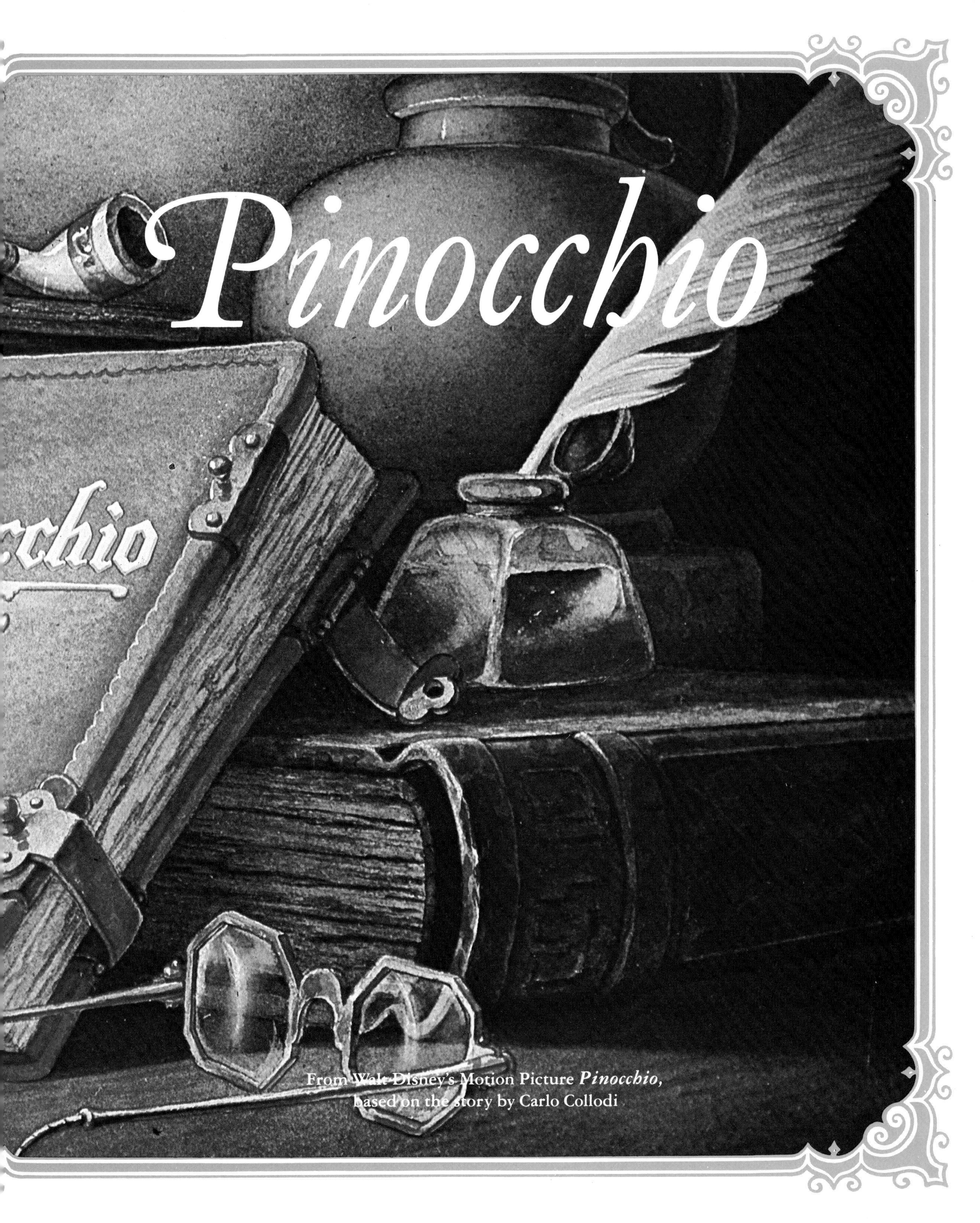

Pinocchio

From Walt Disney's Motion Picture *Pinocchio,*
based on the story by Carlo Collodi

There was once a poor woodcarver named Geppetto who made fantastic clocks and music boxes and every kind of toy you can imagine, each one a work of art. Geppetto, who almost never had enough to eat, thought that if he made a clever wooden puppet that could dance and turn somersaults in the air he could travel around the world with it and earn his bit of bread and glass of wine. So he found a good smooth piece of wood and, taking up his tools, he carved a little boy, painted him in bright colors, and gave him the name of Pinocchio.

The puppet could walk and dance very well if Geppetto pulled its strings. But the woodcarver, who lived a lonely life with only his goldfish, Cleo, and his cat, Figaro, for company, thought, "Wouldn't it be wonderful if Pinocchio was a real boy?" That night when everyone was sound asleep the Blue Fairy came down from her star in the sky and touched Pinocchio with her wand. The puppet's strings disappeared at her touch, while the Blue Fairy recited these words:

Little puppet made of pine,
Wake! The gift of life is thine!

Pinocchio was startled to find that he could move by himself and could even talk. "Am I a real boy?" he asked in amazement. But the fairy explained that to become a real boy he would have to prove himself brave, truthful, and unselfish, and would have to learn to choose between right and wrong. "Then, some day you *will* be a real boy, Pinocchio," she promised.

The Blue Fairy appointed Jiminy Cricket—a talking cricket, who had lived a hundred years and more in the house—to be Pinocchio's conscience and to teach him the difference between right and wrong. As she faded away in the glow of her bright star, her voice drifted back, "Remember, Pinocchio, be a good boy and let your conscience be your guide."

The next morning when he awoke, Geppetto was overjoyed to find that Pinocchio was truly alive. "You must go to school now," he told the puppet, "to learn things and get smart, so you can become a real boy." And the old woodcarver sold his only coat in order to buy Pinocchio schoolbooks and a shiny red apple like the other children's. Pinocchio was so grateful that he threw his arms around Geppetto's neck and thanked him again and again. "I shall learn to read at school today, Father," he promised, and off he skipped, with Jiminy Cricket at his heels.

But on the way to school Pinocchio was stopped by a couple of scheming rascals, J. Worthington Foulfellow, the fox, and his companion Gideon, the alley cat. The minute they laid eyes on the puppet without strings they knew he would be worth a fortune to Stromboli, a showman who owned a traveling puppet theater. "A little wooden boy! What an act!" They convinced Pinocchio that the theater was an easier road to success than school. Jiminy Cricket tried his best to persuade the puppet that he must turn his back on temptation and go to school instead, but Pinocchio, happily trusting his new friends, refused to listen. "Hi-diddle-dee-dee," he sang, "an actor's life for me."

Pinocchio was a great success on the stage, where the audience rained gold and silver coins on him. When Stromboli realized how much money he could make, he placed the valuable puppet in a cage. Pinocchio wept then for his father, Geppetto, and his good conscience, Jiminy, neither of whom he expected ever to see again. But Jiminy Cricket did not give up so easily, and that night he found his way to poor Pinocchio's cage.

While Jiminy was trying to comfort the puppet, the Blue Fairy appeared again. When she asked Pinocchio why he hadn't gone to school, the puppet invented a long story about being kidnapped by two monsters. As he told it, his wooden nose grew longer and longer with each lie, until finally it was like a small tree with branches and leaves sprouting from it.

Pinocchio was frightened. "What's happened?" he asked. "You are telling a lie that keeps growing and growing, as plain as the nose on your face," the fairy replied. Pinocchio promised to be truthful and good from then on, so the Blue Fairy touched his cage with her wand. "This is the last time I can help you," she said, as she freed him. Pinocchio, his nose back to normal, set off to race Jiminy Cricket back to Geppetto's house.

Meanwhile, at the Red Lobster Inn, those two scamps, J. Worthington Foulfellow and Gideon, were plotting new mischief. They had found a wicked coachman who collected stupid little boys who played hooky from school. "I takes 'em to Pleasure Island," he explained, "and they never comes back—as boys." The coachman winked an eye. "I'll pay you a gold piece for every boy you bring me. We leaves at midnight."

Once again Foulfellow and Gideon tricked Pinocchio into going with them. The puppet had been racing Jiminy Cricket home when he met the fox and the cat. They convinced Pinocchio that he needed a vacation at Pleasure Island for the sake of his health, and they personally handed him over to the coachman with the ticket for his fare. With a full load of boys, the coach, pulled by six little donkeys, clattered off to the ferry-boat dock. Luckily Jiminy Cricket had run after Pinocchio and, just in time, he hopped up on the lantern under the coach.

At Pleasure Island Pinocchio became friendly with a tough boy named Lampwick. "This is a great place—no school, you can fight and wreck the place and no one stops you. Take all the cake, pie, dill pickles, and ice cream you want. Stuff yourself. It's all free," Lampwick told him gleefully.

The boys destroyed books and pictures, broke windows, set fire to houses, chopped up furniture, smoked cigars, played cards, and chewed tobacco. "Bein' bad is lots of fun, ain't it?" Pinocchio said to Lampwick, trying to copy the older boy's way of talking. They were playing cards and smoking when Jiminy Cricket finally found Pinocchio. "Look at yourself!" he scolded. "How do you ever expect to be a real boy?"

But Pinocchio was having such a good time he refused to leave when Jiminy asked him. He didn't hear the coachman say to one of his helpers, "Give a bad boy enough rope and he'll soon make a jackass of himself." He didn't see the coachman loading a boat with little donkeys. But Jiminy, who had gone down to the dock alone, saw what was happening. The little donkeys brayed and the coachman cracked his whip at them. "Quiet!" he ordered. "You boys had your fun. Now pay for it!"

Jiminy sped back to Pinocchio. "Hope I'm not too late!" he panted. Lampwick had already been turned into a braying donkey, and Pinocchio had grown donkey's ears and a tail. Jiminy managed to get him to the shore before he got any worse, and the two of them swam for the mainland.

Geppetto, in the meantime, had gone out to search for his missing son. When Pinocchio and Jiminy Cricket finally came to his house it was dark and empty. They were sitting sadly on the curb, wondering what

could have happened to the kindly old man, when a dove dropped a note at their feet. Jiminy read the message aloud—Geppetto, while trying to get to Pleasure Island to find Pinocchio, had been swallowed by Monstro the Whale. He was still alive, in the whale's stomach, at the bottom of the sea.

"I'm going to find him," Pinocchio declared. He set off for the ocean with Jiminy hopping along behind him. "He's a whale of a whale," the cricket warned, "and besides it's dangerous." But Pinocchio was determined to find his father. When they got to the ocean they plunged into the water and swam until they saw the huge dark shape of Monstro.

When the whale opened his jaws, Pinocchio and Jiminy swam into his mouth. There, inside the enormous creature, were Geppetto and his little raft. "Father," cried Pinocchio. "Pinocchio! My son!" Geppetto exclaimed, hugging and kissing the puppet.

Together they figured out how to escape. They built a fire inside the whale and, when the smoke made Monstro sneeze, they were ready on the raft and quickly paddled out of his open mouth. Everything worked according to plan until the enraged whale caught sight of the little raft as it headed for shore. He pursued it and smashed it into splinters with his great tail, knocking Geppetto unconscious. Pinocchio bravely rescued his father and then tried to divert the angry whale while

Geppetto was carried safely to shore by a big wave. After being trapped under some rocks, the puppet was finally washed ashore, half drowned.

Sadly Geppetto carried Pinocchio home and put him to bed. He wiped away a tear as he looked at the donkey ears growing out of Pinocchio's head and thought of how brave the puppet had been. Suddenly the room glowed with bright blue starlight and the Blue Fairy appeared at the bedside. "Awake, Pinocchio, awake!" she said. "You have been brave, truthful, and unselfish."

Pinocchio sat up and opened his eyes. "Father!" he called. "I'm alive!" Then, looking at his hands, he continued, "And I'm real! *I'm a real boy!*" Geppetto, Cleo, and Figaro were overjoyed, and hugged and kissed the good-looking little boy with dark brown hair and blue eyes, who appeared so happy and full of joy.

Jiminy Cricket smiled. "He deserved to be a real boy," he said. At that there appeared on his lapel a badge of solid gold with "Official Conscience" spelled out on its ribbon. "Oh, thank you, Ma'am," the cricket chirped, but the Blue Fairy had already vanished. Only a brilliant star winked at Jiminy, its beams sparkling on his golden badge.

Contentedly the cricket sang his favorite song:

When you wish upon a star
Your dream comes true.

PINOCCHIO

The Story of the Production

How do you follow the outstanding accomplishment of *Snow White and the Seven Dwarfs,* Walt Disney's first feature-length cartoon, which won worldwide audience acceptance and a Special Academy Award in 1939? Why, you start right in on a new feature, embellish the animation, and, in the words of Milt Kahl, one of the animation directors, "Spend money and creative energy like they have never been spent since."

That's what Walt Disney did with his second full-length animated feature, *Pinocchio.* He built up his modest cartoon factory from a staff of three hundred to one of nearly two thousand, and experimented with new techniques with bold self-assurance. The excitement—and money—generated by the success of *Snow White* were lavished on Carlo Collodi's nineteenth-century children's classic about the wooden puppet who became a real boy.

Pinocchio revolutionized animated special effects, paving the way for *Fantasia.* Disney and his artists conceived the impossible, and the technicians created a fairyland of imagination and dramatic visual effects. The picture won two Academy Awards for 1940, the year of its release: Best Original Musical Score and Best Song, "When You Wish Upon a Star," sung by Jiminy Cricket. "Give a Little Whistle," "Little Woodenhead," "Hi-Diddle-Dee-Dee," "I've Got No Strings," and "Turn on the Old Music Box" were the other songs, all of them designed to carry the major story points and advance the action.

Pinocchio has been released on an average of every eight years since its premiere and has attracted a larger audience each time.

Walt Disney and the marionette star of his 1940 feature, *Pinocchio,* seem to be congratulating each other on a superlative production

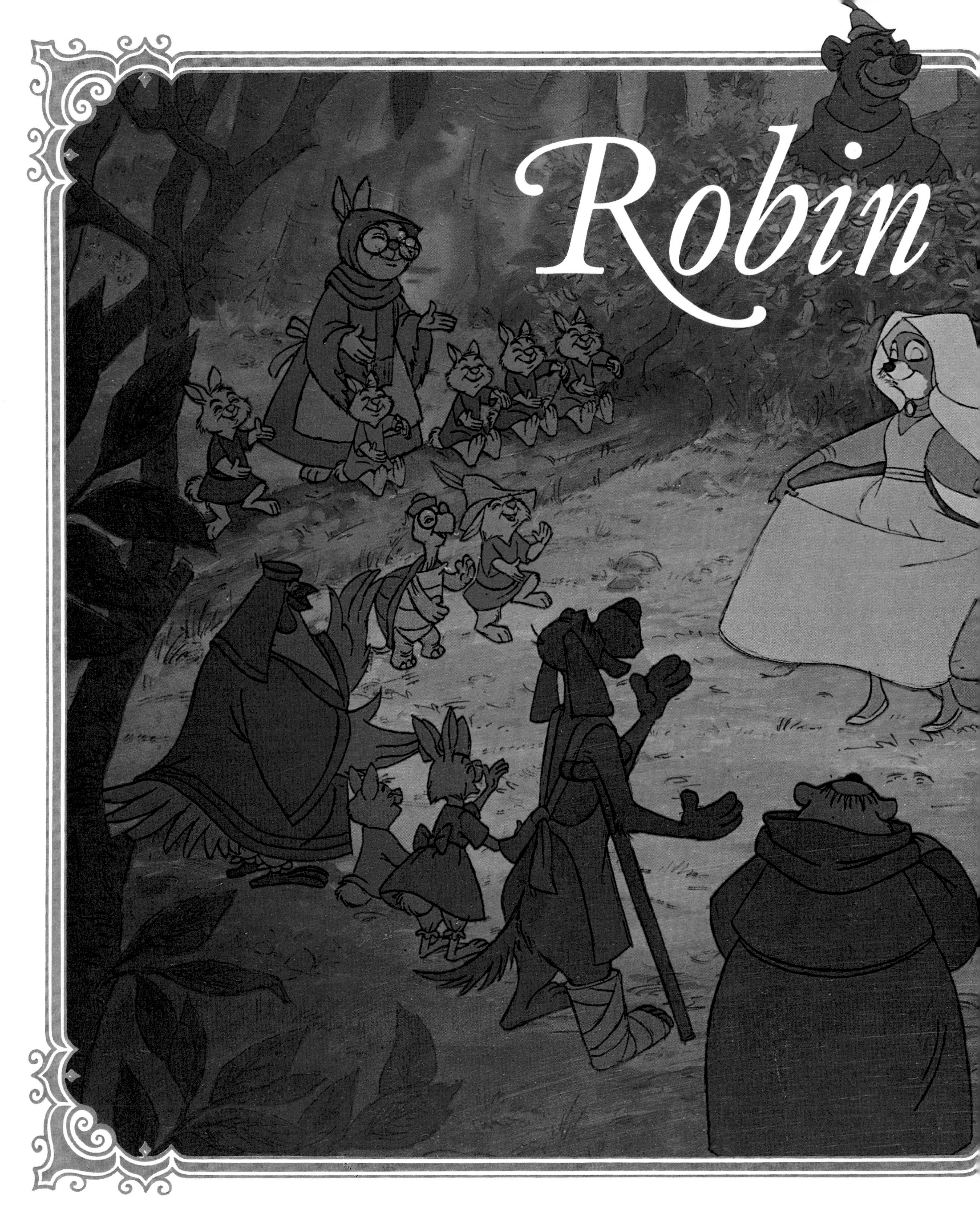
Robin

Hood

From Walt Disney Productions' Motion Picture *Robin Hood*

he animal kingdom has its own version of the Robin Hood legends, the tales of the English hero of the common people, whose adventures were first sung by medieval minstrels. Allan a Dale, a sweet-voiced rooster, who was Robin Hood's favorite singer, presents their version.

One fine spring day, Robin Hood, a clever fox, and Little John, a large bear, were walking through Sherwood Forest, dressed from top to toe in Lincoln green. All the members of Robin's merry band wore Lincoln green and lived deep in Sherwood Forest as outlaws. Yet they were beloved by the country people because none ever came to Robin in time of need and went away empty-handed.

Now the times were troubled because good King Richard had gone off on the Third Crusade, leaving his brother Prince John, a scrawny and tyrannical lion, to rule England. Prince John's chief adviser was Sir Hiss, a wily snake, and between the two of them they had put a heavy burden of taxes on the poor people. This fine spring day, Prince John's

entourage was making its way through Sherwood Forest on the way to Nottingham to tax the people there. As Prince John said to Sir Hiss, "Rob the poor to feed the rich. Am I right, counsellor?" and he and Sir Hiss chuckled gleefully as they fondled the bags of gold they had already collected.

Robin Hood and Little John saw the royal entourage in the distance, and Little John asked, "Are we good guys or bad guys? You know, out robbing the rich to feed the poor?" But Robin Hood

corrected him. "*Rob* is a naughty word. We never rob, we just *borrow* a bit from those who can afford it." Then he pointed to the Royal Coach. "And here comes another collection day for the poor."

The two outlaws quickly slipped into disguises as gypsy fortune tellers, and ran ahead to the side of the road. When the Royal Coach passed, they offered to tell Prince John his fortune. Cleverly, Robin Hood and Little John flattered the Prince and in a very short time they had tricked him out of his jewels, his money bags, and even the royal robes. Then off they scampered into the depths of Sherwood Forest, loaded down with their loot.

Prince John was furious upon discovering that he had been tricked, and when he arrived at Nottingham he wanted revenge. His helpless subjects paid dearly for his humiliation. He taxed the heart and soul out of the poor people of Nottingham, and if they couldn't pay, they were carted off to jail. But most of all, Prince John wanted to catch that scalawag Robin Hood and punish him.

He told the Sheriff of Nottingham, a villainous wolf, to announce an archery tournament with the first prize a golden arrow and a kiss from his niece Maid Marian, a beautiful vixen. Prince John knew that Robin Hood had loved Marian a long time ago, before he became an outlaw, and he was sure that such a prize would lure Robin out of his hiding place.

Nottingham was a fair sight on the day of the archery match. All along the green meadow outside the town wall stretched rows of benches for people of rank and quality. At the end of the range, near the target, was a raised platform bedecked with ribbons, pennants, and garlands of flowers for the Prince, Maid Marian, and the royal party. The poorer folk sat or lay upon the green grass near the railing that kept them off the archery range. The very best archers of Merry England had come to this shooting match, and they gathered in the great tent, inspecting their bows and arrows and talking of the good shots they had made in their day. The Sheriff looked about for Robin Hood, but did not see him among the archers. "He is too big a coward to appear," he thought.

But the Sheriff was mistaken. Robin, who was one of the best archers in England, would not have missed this tournament for all the world. He and his Merry Men were there in various disguises, mingling with the crowd. Some were friars, some beggars, some peasants; Robin himself was a stork, while Little John got himself up as the Duke of Chutney and sat on the royal platform at Prince John's left hand.

The tournament had narrowed down to two contestants, the Sheriff of Nottingham and a talkative stork who spoke every time the Sheriff was about to make his shot. "Listen, Scissorbill, if you shoot half as good as you blabbermouth, you're better'n Robin Hood," said the irritated Sheriff. "He's scared of me. That's why he didn't show up today." Then the Sheriff shot his last arrow and it went straight to the bull's-eye. He was certain he had won the contest. But the stork had one more arrow and, drawing his trusty bow, he loosed the string. The arrow flew so true that it knocked the Sheriff's arrow off the target and lodged dead center in the bull's-eye.

The stork strode confidently up to the royal platform to receive his prize. But Prince John knew there was only one archer in all the land who could shoot like that. He tapped the stork on each shoulder with his sword, causing the disguise to fall away. "I sentence you to instant and immediate death, Robin Hood!" proclaimed Prince John. The Sheriff and the executioner seized the outlaw and bound him with stout ropes. Maid Marian pleaded for his life in vain, and all of his friends were in despair—when suddenly the Prince said, "Let him go!" Little John, as the Duke of Chutney, had quietly put his knife to the Prince's back and forced him to withdraw his orders.

Then the Merry Men of Sherwood came forward out of the crowd and battled with the royal guards. In the confusion Robin escaped with Maid Marian. They made their way to the hiding place deep in Sherwood Forest, and when all the band was together again the forest rang with their songs and laughter as they waited for the day when good King Richard would return to England and reclaim the throne from his unjust brother.

Once again an enraged Prince John, advised by Sir Hiss, punished the people with taxes four times greater than before. Soon the prisons were filled with poor people unable to pay, among them Robin's friend, kindly Friar Tuck, a badger. Once again, hoping to lure Robin Hood out into the open, the Prince set a trap. He announced that he would hang the good Friar for treason the very next morning. Secretly he hoped it would prove to be a double hanging, for surely Robin would come to Nottingham to save his friend, and this time they would be ready for him.

Robin and Little John stole into the town late at night. "A jailbreak is the only chance he's got," Robin Hood decided. Silently Little John crept up behind the sentry, who had just called out the time and his "All is well." Little John pulled him over the castle wall, where Robin Hood took his keys and donned his uniform. They tiptoed past the Sheriff of Nottingham, who was snoozing at the prison gate, and in short order they unlocked all the barred doors and freed the villagers who were imprisoned.

"I'll just drop in on the royal treasury, for good measure," Robin said. He tossed a hook and rope to the balcony of Prince John's bedchamber and shinnied his way up. From the balcony he shot an arrow, attached to a rope, through a prison window where Little John waited. Little John threaded the rope through an iron ring and shot it back to Robin Hood, making a perfect double clothesline and pulley. Then Little John sat back to wait for the fun.

Cautiously Robin Hood entered Prince John's chambers, where the Prince and Sir Hiss were snoring in their beds. Bags of gold were everywhere, even under the Prince's pillow. Robin stealthily removed them, one by one, to the balcony. There he fastened them to the

clothesline, and Little John then reeled them toward himself at the window of the jail. Friar Tuck helped pull the bags in, chuckling, "Praise the Lord and pass the tax rebate." Soon all the freed villagers were loaded down with gold. Led by Little John and Friar Tuck, they marched out of the jail in the dawn's first light, past the empty gallows that Robin Hood had helped them to cheat.

Robin took the last two bags of gold, leapt from the balcony to the clothesline, and rode off on it. Sir Hiss and Prince John awakened just as Robin fled, and Sir Hiss tried to recapture the last bag of gold. When he pulled at it, it split open, showering coins down on the villagers below, who happily ran off with them.

The Prince and Sir Hiss were strung out on the clothesline, screaming for help. Their cries alerted the guards, who charged after Robin, but he was too fast and clever for them. Meanwhile, Little John, the Friar, and the villagers clambered onto a two-wheeled cart and crossed the drawbridge just in time. Robin Hood held off the guards and then dived from the palace wall into the moat, where no one dared follow him. It was a time of narrow escapes and wild excitement, not soon forgotten in the town of Nottingham.

But, all's well that ends well. King Richard, a lion-hearted lion, returned from the Crusade and set his kingdom straight. Maid Marian and Robin Hood were married (the King joked that he had an outlaw for an in-law) and went to live quietly and lawfully in Sherwood Forest. And as for Prince John, Sir Hiss, and the Sheriff of Nottingham, they too found a new home—in the Nottingham prison.

Royal
Rock Pile

ROBIN HOOD

The Story of the Production

In this, the first cartoon feature conceived and created without Walt Disney, the talented team he had forged at the Studio carried his work forward. While *The Aristocats* was still being drawn, Ken Anderson, art director and developer of new projects, scouted stories for the next feature, which was to be taken from the classics.

Robin Hood was the choice, but it was given a unique "unclassic" twist worthy of Walt Disney himself. Wolfgang (Woolie) Reitherman, the producer-director, pointed out that this version of the age-old tale is presented "as seen through the eyes of the animals of Sherwood Forest who knew Robin best." This unusual gambit had the double virtue of originality and practicality—playing to the greatest strength of the Studio artists, who drew animals with human foibles superlatively well.

So we find the Disney Robin Hood a bold and crafty fox, Little John a large, fun-loving bear, Prince John a neurotic lion, Sir Hiss (a pure Disney invention who didn't exist in the original Robin Hood tales) a sycophantic snake, the Sheriff of Nottingham a villainous wolf, Friar Tuck a badger, and Maid Marian a lovely vixen. The voices for the characters were supplied by actors whose gestures and mannerisms added immeasurably to the personalities as they took shape on the drawing boards. The characteristics of Peter Ustinov himself lurk behind the expressions and movements of Prince John; Phil Harris, who was the happy-go-lucky Baloo in *The Jungle Book* and O'Malley in *The Aristocats,* lends his voice and personality to Little John; Terry-Thomas, the gap-toothed British comedian, used his distinctive sibilance for Sir Hiss; Andy Devine of the gravel voice spoke for Friar Tuck; and Brian Bedford, a British Hamlet, was the polished, sophisticated voice of Robin Hood.

Describing the conditions under which the Disney team worked, Reitherman explained, "The atmosphere in the Studio was alive with creativity, a marriage of many minds and talents. From our imagination we created frame-by-frame spontaneity. We've sustained that feeling through many cartoon features from *Snow White* to *Robin Hood* because no picture has ever been the same. We were always trying new methods, new techniques, pioneering one thing or another."

Robin Hood, released in 1972, was a worthy successor to the animated features previously created under Walt Disney's personal supervision.

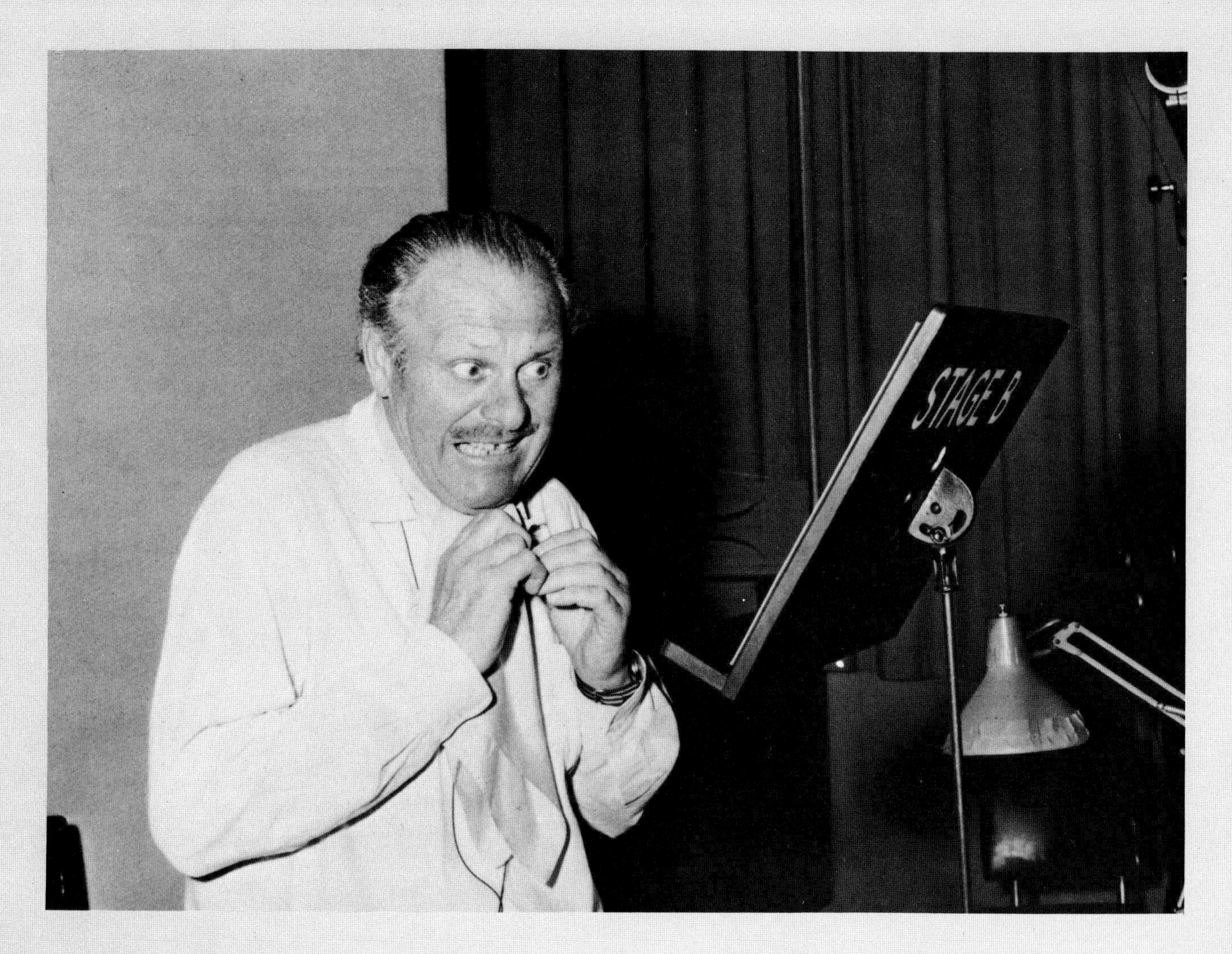

Terry-Thomas becomes the crafty villain as he records the voice of Sir Hiss, the sly snake

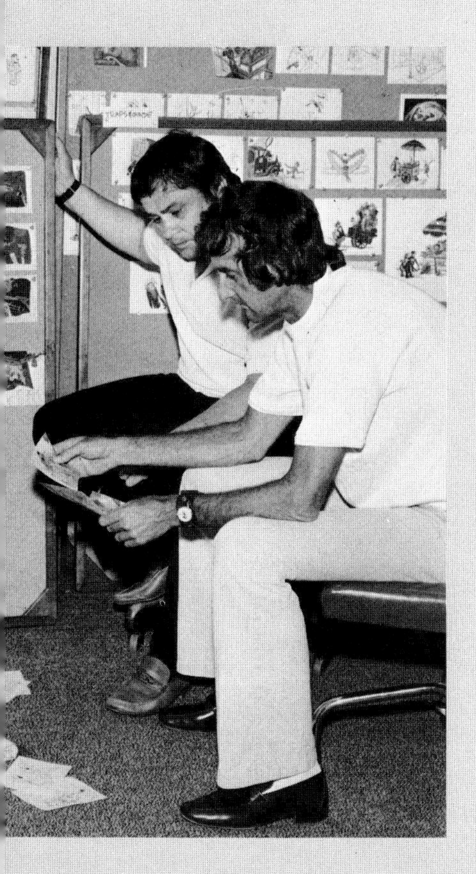

Art director Ken Anderson and two assistants decide on set and character designs

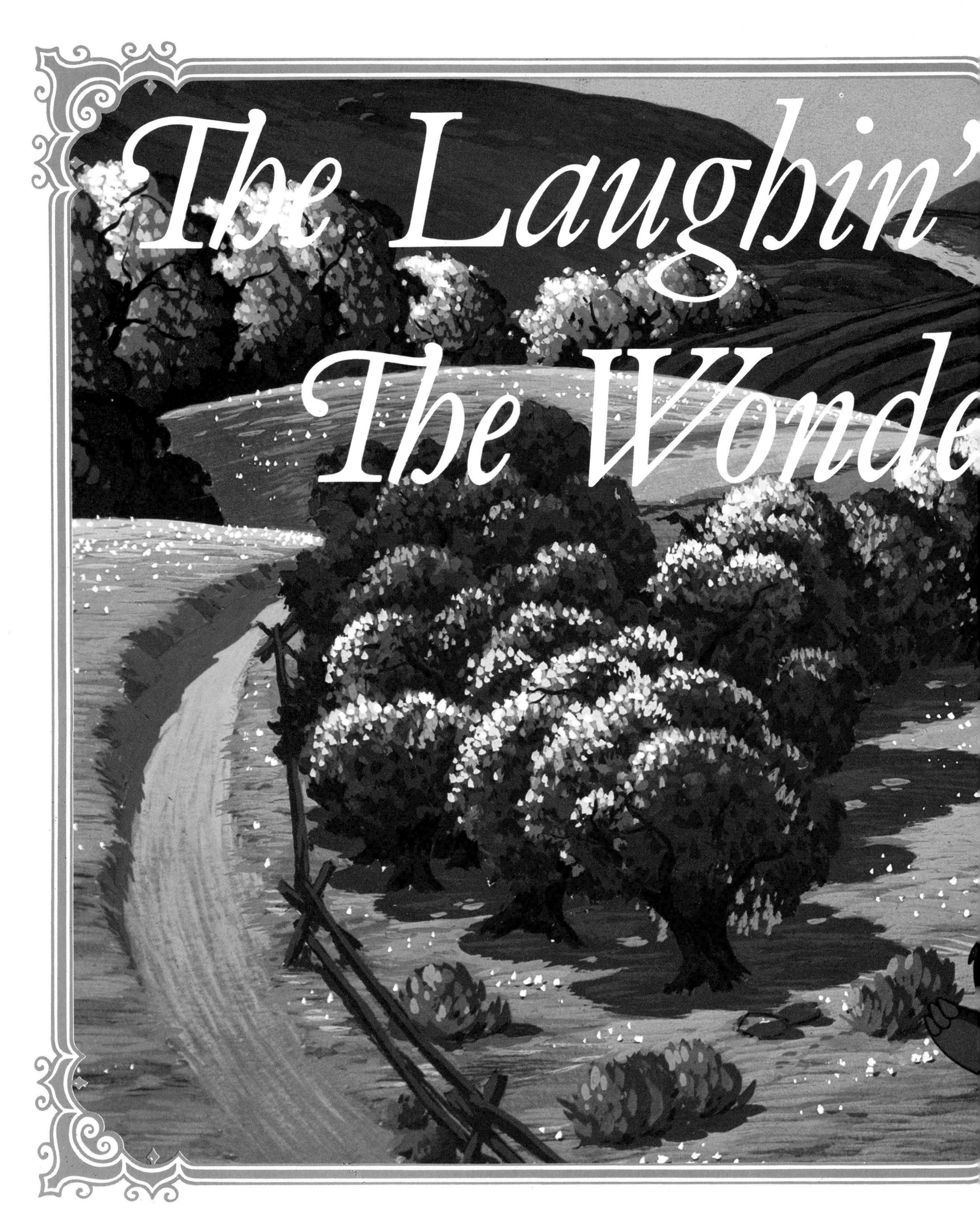

The Laughin'
The Wonde

Place AND
rful Tar-Baby

Adapted from Walt Disney's Motion Picture *Song of the South,*
based on the *Tales of Uncle Remus* by Joel Chandler Harris

idn't the fox *ever* catch the rabbit, Uncle Remus?" asked Johnny one evening. "He come mighty near to, honey; he an' Brer Bear," said Uncle Remus. "You jes' set an' listen an' I'll tell you."

One day Brer Bear wuz walkin' along near Chickapin Hill at de edge o' de big woods, carryin' his club over his shoulder an' a-hopin' he'd meet up wid Brer Rabbit. Cuz he kinda fancied some barbeque rabbit fur his dinner. Sho' enuf, he caught dat smart rabbit nappin' an' he whopped him a good one wif his club. Brer Rabbit he saw stars, an' next thing he know he is in Brer Fox's cave, all tied up on a barbeque spit. Brer Fox is fixin' a big fire while Brer Bear is holdin' Brer Rabbit an' thinkin' what a good dinner he's gonna be.

'Stead o' bein' sceered, Brer Rabbit starts to laugh, real hard. Dat make Brer Fox angry an' he sez, "I'se gonna roast you on dat fire! Is dat somethin' to laugh about?" But Brer Rabbit he jes' laugh louder. An' he sez, "I can't help laughin' cuz I jes' been to my laughin' place."

Well, Brer Bear he gotta laugh too, an' Brer Fox likewise. "What's a laughin' place?" dey want to know. "Oh," sez Brer Rabbit, "jes' a secret place I knows about." "Where's dis laughin' place at?" Brer Bear asks. "How can I show you when I'se all tied up like dis?" de rabbit answers, very cocky.

So, next thing you know, Brer Bear untie Brer Rabbit from de spit but keep holt of de rope so's he can lead 'em to de laughin' place. "It's another of dat rabbit's tricks," sez Brer Fox, but Brer Bear sez, "I'm de one dat cotched him, an' I wanna see dat laughin' place."

Brer Rabbit, he lead 'em to a clump of bushes an' sez, "In dere." Brer Bear an' Brer Fox goes in, an' when dey come runnin' out dey is covered with bees. Dey let go Brer Rabbit's rope and away dey run. But

Brer Fox he yell, "I'll git you for dis, you smart-alecky rabbit." Brer Rabbit, he laugh fit to kill. "I didn't say it wuz *yo'* laughin' place. I said it wuz *my* laughin' place, Brer Fox."

But Brer Rabbit he worried dat Brer Fox and Brer Bear dey are shore out to git him dis time. He nails up de door of his house in de ole briar patch an' heads fo' some new place where dere ain't gonna be no trouble. An' off he hop down de road, lippity-clippity, clippity-lippity, jes' as sassy as a jay-bird, a-singin':

> Zip-a-dee-doo-dah,
> Zip-a-dee-ay,
> Plenty of sunshine
> Headin' my way.

Brer Fox an' Brer Bear dey angry 'bout bein' fooled agin by Brer Rabbit, an' dey goes ter work and gets dem some tar. Dey fix up a contrapshun wat dey called a Tar-Baby. An' dey tuck dis here Tar-Baby an' sot him in de big road.

Dey didn't have ter wait long, cuz bimeby along come Brer Rabbit. Brer Fox an' Brer Bear dey lay low. Brer Rabbit spy de Tar-Baby an' jump up on his behime legs like he wuz 'stonished. De Tar-Baby, he sot dere. "Mawnin'!" sez Brer Rabbit. "Nice wedder diz mawnin'." Tar-Baby ain't sayin' nothin' an' Brer Fox wink his eye slow at Brer Bear an' dey bofe lay low. "Oh, I hope he hit 'im!" say Brer Fox.

Brer Rabbit raise his voice. "Is you deaf? Cuz if you is, I kin holler louder," sez he.

Tar-Baby stay still an' Brer Fox an' Brer Bear, dey lay low.

Brer Rabbit 'lows it's up to him to teach de stuck-up stranger some manners, an' he sez, "Look, if hits de las' thing I does, I'm gwineter learn you how to talk ter 'spectable folks. If you don't take off dat hat an' tell me howdy, I'm gwineter bus' you wide open," sez he.

Tar-Baby stay still an' Brer Fox an' Brer Bear dey lay low—wid de fidgets.

Brer Rabbit kep on axin' him an' de Tar-Baby kep sayin' nothin' an' finally Brer Rabbit draw back wid his fis' an' blip, he hit de side of the Tar-Baby's head. Right dar is where he broke his molasses jug. His fis' stuck an' he cain't pull loose. "Leggo my fis'!" he holler. "Ef you don't let me loose, I'll hit you agin," an' wid dat he fotch him a swipe wid de udder han' an' dat stuck too. Tar-Baby, he ain't sayin' nothin', an' Brer Fox an' Brer Bear lay low. Den Brer Rabbit he hit, kick, butt wif his haid till he tarred all over, only his eyes showin'.

Den Brer Fox an' Brer Bear, dey sauntered out, whistlin' an' lookin' innocent. Dey do a little shuffle an' dance. "Howdy, Brer Rabbit," sez Brer Fox. "You sho' look all stuck up dis mawnin'!" Den dey roll on de groun' an' laugh. "I speck you'll take dinner wid us dis time. We ain't gwineter take no excuse like de lass time," sez Brer Bear.

"Well, I speck I got you dis time, Brer Rabbit," sez Brer Fox. "You been sassin' me an' trickin' me a long time. Now dar you is an' dar you stay while I sharpen my axe for to skin you." Brer Rabbit he smart, an' if he ever gwineter use his head, now's the time to do it.

"Skin me, Brer Fox," sez Brer Rabbit. "Snatch out my eyeballs, roast me, but don't, please, Brer Fox, don't fling me in dat briar patch," sez he.

Brer Fox an' Brer Bear wants to hurt Brer Rabbit bad ez dey can. "Maybe I'll hang him," sez Brer Fox, "if I can fine me some string." "Hang me, if you like, go ahead, but don't throw me in dat briar patch," sez Brer Rabbit, lookin' mighty skeered of de sharp thorns an' brambles.

"We wouldn't do dat," sez Brer Fox. "No sir, we wouldn't do dat," sez Brer Bear, an' dey cotched him by de behime legs an' slung him right in the middle of de briar patch.

Brer Rabbit yelled and hollered. Dere was a flutterin' of leaves in de bushes, an' when Brer Fox take a peek, dere lie po' Brer Rabbit wid a lily on his chest. But he only playin' dead. Bimeby Brer Fox an' Brer Bear hear someone jumpin' roun' in dat briar patch and hoppin' through it way up de hill. "Born an' bred in de briar patch, Brer Fox—born an' bred in de briar patch!" Brer Rabbit call. An' wid dat Brer Rabbit skip off as lively as a cricket.

SONG OF THE SOUTH

The Story of the Production

As a boy Walt Disney had enjoyed *The Tales of Uncle Remus* by Joel Chandler Harris, and the idea of making a film based on the hilarious adventures of Brer Rabbit, Brer Bear, Brer Fox, and the other denizens of the Briar Patch had appealed to him for a long time. He envisioned Uncle Remus and the children for whom he spun his yarns as flesh-and-blood characters, while the animals and their adventures would be ideal subjects for animation. From the dozens of Uncle Remus stories Disney chose "The Wonderful Tar-Baby," "The Laughing Place," and "Running Away" to be animated in *Song of the South.*

Set in a vanished past—"Not in your day, nor yet in my day," says Uncle Remus, "but once upon a time"—the motion picture takes place in the antebellum South where a lonely, frightened little boy finds solace in wise old Uncle Remus and his humorously apt but timeless fables.

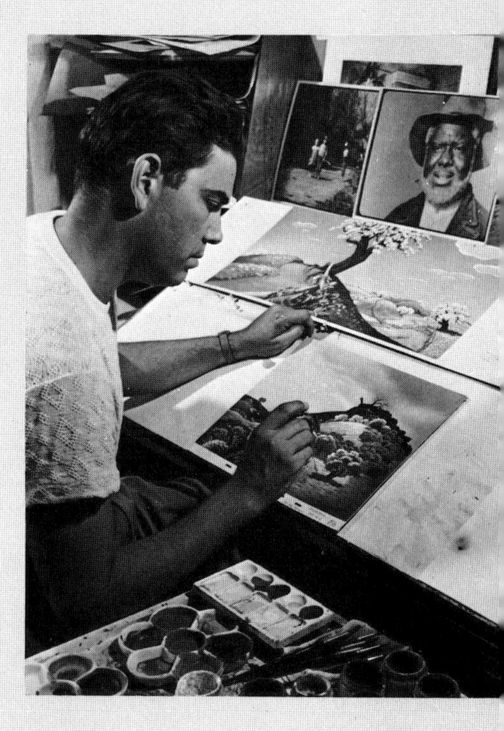

A photograph of James Baskett, the Uncle Remus of the live-action portion of *Song of the South,* faces a Disney artist painting a scene for the animated stories in the film

Two years in the making, *Song of the South* was released in 1946 as a full-length (one hour and thirty-five minutes) musical production with the Academy Award–winning "Zip-A-Dee-Doo-Dah" the most popular of its ten songs. The cast of live actors featured James Baskett, in his first screen appearance, as Uncle Remus. A former entertainer in vaudeville, chautauqua, and tent shows, Baskett was awarded a special Oscar "for his able and heart-warming characterization of Uncle Remus, friend and storyteller to the children of the world." His was also the voice of the sly Brer Fox. Ruth Warrick, Bobby Driscoll, Lucile Watson, and Hattie McDaniel were among the other members of the cast.

Joel Chandler Harris began collecting what he called his "plantation fables" nearly a hundred years ago. These deceptively simple folk tales interested him, he explained, "because of the unadulterated human nature that might be found in them." The stories have helped generations of youngsters understand themselves and the world about them, and today are considered classics of their kind. They have been translated into eighteen languages. To give Uncle Remus himself the final word, "If dey don't do good, how come dey last so long?"

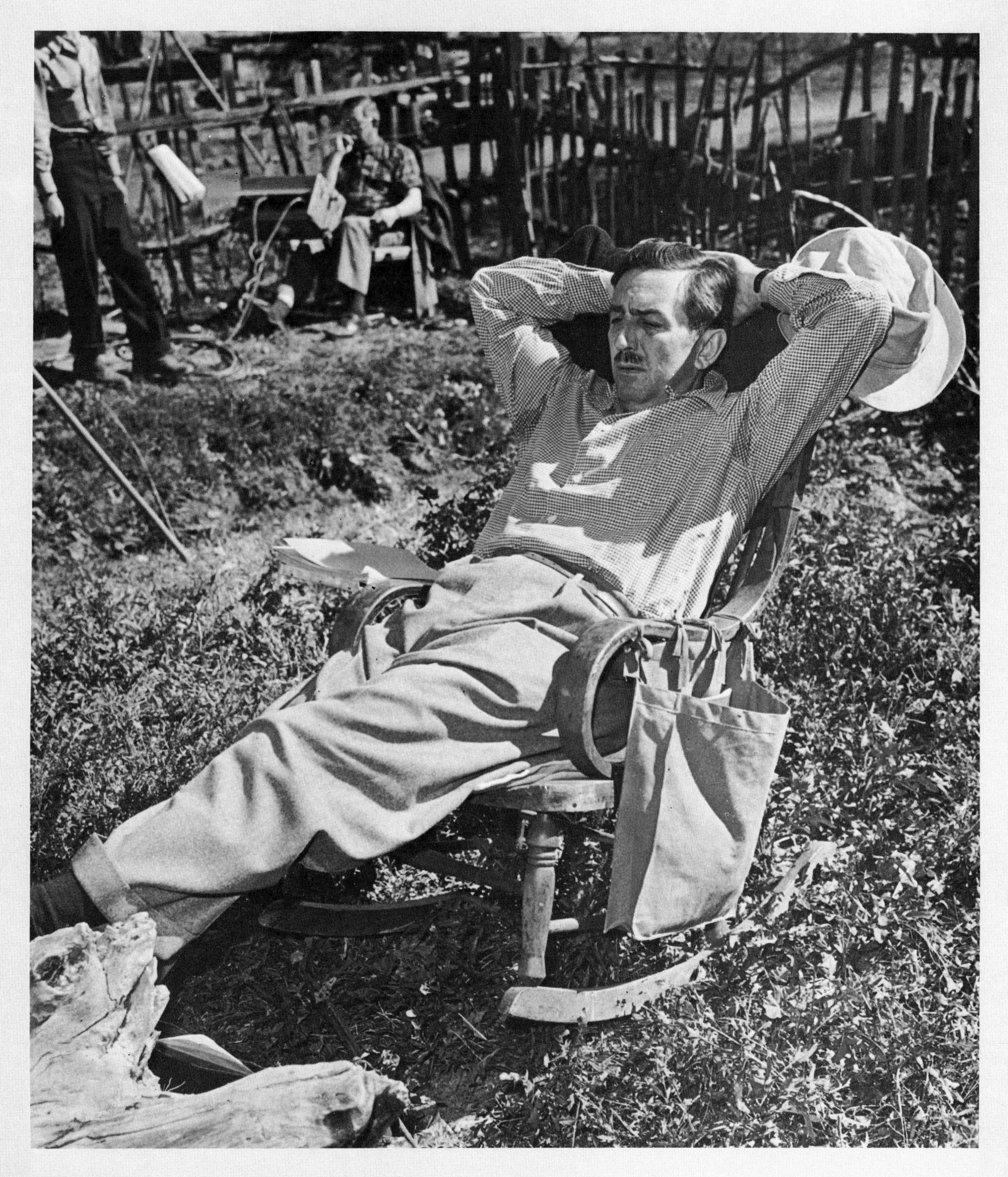

Walt Disney, on location, unwinds in Uncle Remus' rocking chair

Ichabod Crane

From Walt Disney's Motion Picture *The Legend of Sleepy Hollow,*
based on the original story by Washington Irving

f we could journey back to that time in American history when Manhattan was but a Dutch market town, we would discover in the bosom of one of those spacious coves which indent the eastern shore of the Hudson River a small rural port generally known by the name of Tarry Town. This name was given in former days by the good housewives of the countryside because of the natural inclination of their husbands to tarry about the village tavern on market days.

About two miles from this village there is a little valley among high hills which is one of the quietest places in the whole world. This sequestered glen has long been known as Sleepy Hollow, and its rustic lads are called the Sleepy Hollow Boys throughout the neighboring country. A drowsy, dreamy influence seems to hang over the land. Some say the place was bewitched in the early days. The whole neighborhood abounds with haunted spots, strange sights, and twilight superstitions. The dominant spirit that haunts this enchanted region is the apparition of a figure on horseback without a head, who has sometimes been seen by the country folk galloping along in the gloom of night as if on the wings of the wind. This specter is known as the Headless Horseman of Sleepy Hollow.

Into this quiet valley there came, late one drowsy autumn afternoon, an itinerant schoolmaster from Connecticut, by name of Ichabod Crane. To see him strolling along with his coat flapping and fluttering around him, one might well mistake him for some scarecrow escaped from a cornfield. He was tall and exceedingly lank; his head was small and flat on top with a long, pointed nose that looked like a weather vane perched on his spindle neck.

As Ichabod walked down the main street of the village reading a book, the townspeople were astonished at the sight of their new schoolmaster, but they soon found that he did his work well. He ruled over the children in his one-room schoolhouse by bearing in mind the golden maxim, "Spare the rod and spoil the child." Ichabod Crane's scholars certainly were not spoiled.

But after school he was the companion and playmate of the children, and would even walk some of the smaller ones home, especially if they happened to have pretty sisters or mothers noted for their good cooking.

According to country custom in those parts, Ichabod boarded and lodged at the houses of the farmers whose children he instructed. He lived with each family a week, and went the rounds of the neighborhood with all his worldly goods tied up in a large cotton handkerchief.

Ichabod found other ways to increase his slender income—he was the singing master of the neighborhood and taught the young people to sing psalms. On Sundays, when he led the choir, his nasal voice resounded far above all the rest of the congregation. There are peculiar quavers still heard in that church and even half a mile off on a still Sunday morning, which are said to be descended from the nose of Ichabod Crane.

The females of the neighborhood found the schoolmaster to be vastly superior in taste and accomplishments to the rough Sleepy Hollow Boys and their leader, Brom Bones. Ichabod was invited to tea at the farmhouses, or would take a Sunday stroll with a whole bevy of country damsels along the banks of the millpond while the more bashful country bumpkins hung sheepishly back, envying him.

It was inevitable that Ichabod would become an object of ridicule to Brom Bones and his friends, but he didn't mind. He was content in the women's admiration of his great learning, for he had read several books quite through and was a perfect master of Cotton Mather's *History of New England Witchcraft,* in which, by the way, he most firmly believed.

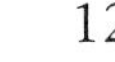

There came a time, however, when the teacher's path was crossed by a being that causes more perplexity to mortal man than ghosts and goblins. That being was a woman, Katrina Van Tassel, the eighteen-year-old daughter and only child of old Baltus Van Tassel, the wealthiest farmer in the county. She was a blooming lass, plump as a partridge, ripe, melting, and rosy-cheeked. And a coquette.

Now there was no doubt that the fair Katrina was the richest prize in the countryside. And the schoolmaster, being an ambitious man, at once began to fill his mind with hopeful suppositions.

"Ah, Katrina, my love, my treasure," he sang to himself, "who can resist your grace, your charm? And who can resist your father's farm?"

From the moment Ichabod decided to gain Katrina's affections his peace of mind was at an end. He had more real difficulties than a knight-errant of yore who had only giants, dragons, enchanters and suchlike to contend with. Ichabod had to win his way to the heart of a country flirt who was surrounded by a number of rustic admirers, including the most formidable obstacle of all—Brom Bones himself. Brom was famed for his great skill in horsemanship, being as dexterous on horseback as a Tartar. He was foremost at all races and cockfights and, with the leadership that bodily strength confers in rustic life, he was the umpire in all disputes. He was always ready either for a fight or a frolic, but had more mischief than ill will in his makeup. And with all his overbearing roughness, there was a strong dash of waggish good humor at bottom.

Such was the rival with whom Ichabod Crane had to contend. Brom had cleared the field of all other suitors and the fair Katrina often wished some champion would appear and, for once, take the field openly against the boisterous Brom, if only because competition would lend some spice to the courtship. And so she did not altogether discourage the schoolteacher's attentions.

In this way, matters went on for some time. It was upon the occasion of her father's annual Halloween frolic that Katrina chose to stir up the embers of the smouldering rivalry. Thus, one invitation in particular carried a most personal and provocative summons.

The gallant Ichabod was in a transport of joy. To him this invitation could mean but one thing. He spent at least an extra half hour at his toilet, brushing and furbishing up his best—and indeed only—suit of rusty black, and admiring himself in a bit of broken looking glass that hung in the schoolhouse. "Just be your own charming self and the fair Katrina is yours for the asking," he told his reflection. So, gaily bedecked and nobly mounted on a broken-down plowhorse he had borrowed for the occasion, Ichabod rode forth like a knight of old to keep a tryst with his lady fair.

In all the countryside there was nothing to equal a merrymaking at Mynheer Van Tassel's farm. Neighbors from miles around, dressed in their best, came to partake of the ample charms of a genuine Dutch country tea-table in the sumptuous time of autumn. Such heaped-up platters of cakes of various kinds known only to experienced Dutch housewives! There was the doughnut, the crisp and crumbling cruller, sweet cakes and shortcakes, ginger cakes and honey cakes—a whole family of cakes. And then there were apple pies, peach pies, and pumpkin pies, besides slices of ham and smoked beef; and, moreover, delectable dishes of preserved plums and peaches and pears and quinces; not to mention broiled shad and roasted chicken; and with the motherly teapot sending up its clouds of vapor from the midst. Ichabod Crane did ample justice to every dainty.

The sound of music from the common room summoned all to the dance. Ichabod prided himself on his dancing as much as upon his singing voice. Not a limb was idle, and to have seen his loose frame clattering about the room you would have thought Saint Vitus himself, that blessed patron of the dance, was cutting the figures before you in person. The lady of his heart was his partner while Brom Bones, sorely smitten with love and jealousy, sat brooding by himself in a corner.

There was no doubt that Ichabod was the man of the hour, but Brom Bones was a stubborn suitor and was determined that, by fair means or foul, his time would come.

When the night grew late, Van Tassel always called upon his guests to tell ghostly tales of Halloween. Brom knew there was no more firm believer in spooks and goblins than Ichabod Crane, and he moved close to the teacher and began to tell a fearsome story of his midnight

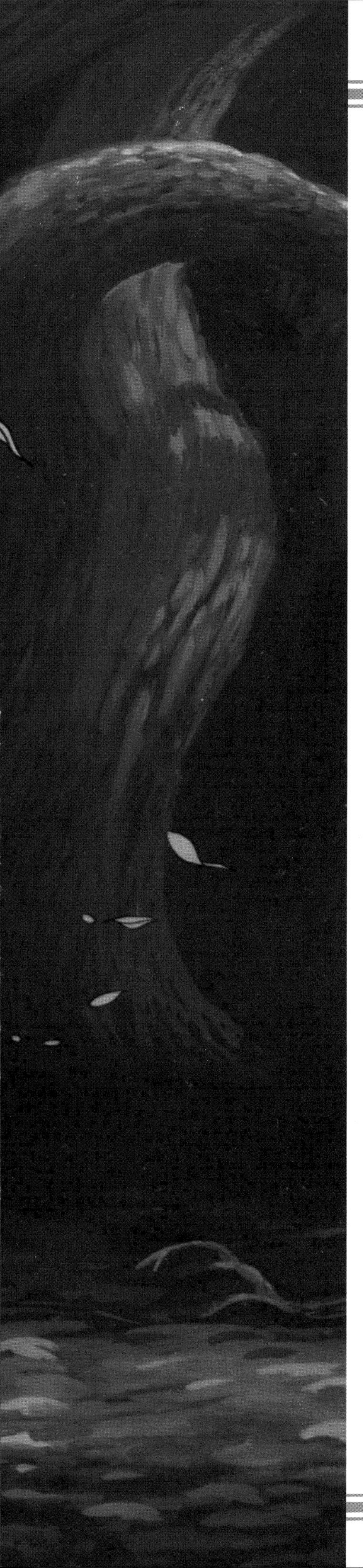

adventure with the Headless Horseman. Ichabod listened with eyes popping as Brom told of being pursued by the Horseman, who was looking for a head to replace his own. Dramatically, Brom finished his tale:

> Now if you doubt this tale is so, I met this spook just a year ago, and I didn't stop for a second look, but made for the bridge that spans the brook; for once you cross that bridge, my friends, the ghost is through—his power ends.

Laughing at the terrified teacher, Brom continued, "So when you're riding home tonight, look out! Beware! Make for the bridge with all your might because the Headless Horseman will be down near the hollow, looking for a head to take."

The party now gradually broke up. The farmers gathered their families in their wagons, and some of the girls left on horseback with their favorite young men. Only Ichabod lingered behind, according to the custom of country lovers, to have a moment alone with the heiress, fully convinced he was now on the high road to success. What was said between them no one knows, but something must have gone wrong, for Ichabod came out after a very short time looking quite unhappy and discouraged. Had the girl only been playing one of her coquettish tricks, encouraging the poor teacher in order to speed the conquest of his rival?

Looking neither to the right or left to gloat over Van Tassel's rich barns and fields, which he had so often dreamed of owning, Ichabod went straight to the stable. With several hearty cuffs and kicks he roused his old horse, who had been soundly sleeping, dreaming of mountains of corn and oats and whole valleys of timothy and clover.

It was at the very witching hour of night that Ichabod pursued his travel homeward. The sky grew blacker as, one by one, the stars winked out and driving clouds obscured the moon. Never had the schoolmaster felt so melancholy, so utterly alone. And the nearer he approached the hollow the more dismal he became.

Once inside the murky glen, Ichabod felt more afraid, for now the forest seemed to close in behind him and every detail of Brom's story returned to haunt him. He tried to whistle a song, but the blowing leaves, an owl's whoo-whoo, the croaking of a frog warning "Headless Horseman, Headless Horseman," filled him with terror. And then he heard the sound of hooves in the distance, coming closer. Suddenly there was wild laughter, and a black horse carrying a headless rider reared up beside him. Ichabod's terror increased when he saw that the head, which should have rested on the rider's shoulders, was carried before him

instead. A sword whizzed past his ear. Ichabod's old horse ran as fast as he could with the other pursuing him. Once again the terrible rider slashed at Ichabod's head with his sword. "If I can but reach that bridge," thought Ichabod, "I am safe."

A convulsive kick in the ribs and the old nag sprang upon the bridge, thundered over the resounding planks, and gained the opposite side. And now Ichabod cast a look behind to see if his ghostly pursuer had vanished. Just then, to his horror, he saw the headless rider rise in his stirrups and hurl the grinning head at him. Ichabod tried to dodge the horrible missile, but too late. It hit his head, tumbling him from his horse.

The next morning they found the old horse cropping grass near his master's gate, but not a trace of the schoolteacher. On the far side of the bridge, however, there was discovered the hat of the unfortunate Ichabod, and close beside it—a shattered pumpkin.

It was shortly thereafter that Brom Bones led the blooming Katrina to the altar. Now rumors persisted that Ichabod still lived, married to a wealthy woman in a distant county. But of course the old country wives, who are the best judges of such matters, refused to believe such nonsense. They knew the schoolmaster had been spirited away by the Headless Horseman, and it is a favorite story often told in the neighborhood round the winter evening fire. Even today, a plowboy, loitering homeward on a still autumn evening, has sometimes thought he heard a voice in the distance chanting a melancholy psalm in the tranquil solitude of Sleepy Hollow.

THE ADVENTURES OF ICHABOD AND MR. TOAD

The Story of the Production

Walt Disney, the master of entertainment, combined a colonial American folk tale, Washington Irving's *Legend of Sleepy Hollow,* with a droll British fantasy, Kenneth Grahame's *Wind in the Willows,* to make a rousingly successful animated feature. Bing Crosby narrated and sang the tale of the ludicrous Yankee schoolmaster, Ichabod Crane, and his devastating courtship. Basil Rathbone, crisply British, told of the reckless capers of Mr. Toad of Toad Hall.

To capture the authentic feeling of the Hudson Valley country and the traditions of a colonial farming community like the one at Sleepy Hollow, Disney personally visited the region around Tarrytown. The results of his careful research can be seen in the accurate details of costumes, buildings, and landscape rendered by the animation artists.

But the Disney version of *Ichabod* is more than the tale of a playful yokel who uses a fearful legend to get the best of his rival for the hand of the local belle. Brom Bones, a hulking but harmless jokester, becomes a menacing demon on his wild midnight chase after the terrified schoolteacher. In those scenes he is a match for any of the most fiendish Disney villains. The dark scarlets, fierce purples, and livid magentas of the Headless Horseman chase scenes raise the emotional pitch—color in action being used in a masterly fashion to heighten the drama.

The Adventures of Ichabod and Mr. Toad was released in 1949. Bing Crosby and his Rhythmaires sang three songs, "Katrina," a sweet ballad; "Ichabod," a light, rhythmic chant; and "Headless Horseman," a fantastic jitter-song very popular on Halloween.

In 1978 Ichabod's story was re-released as *The Legend of Sleepy Hollow.*

The hands of animator Frank Thomas creating the character of Ichabod in action-packed line drawings

Painting a cel is delicate work. No smudges, specks, or fingerprints can mar the celluloid sheet, and the execution must be meticulous because the slightest flaw will be magnified enormously on the motion picture screen

Adapted from the Walt Disney Motion Picture *Peter Pan,*
based upon *Peter Pan* by Sir James Matthew Barrie, by arrangement
with The Hospital for Sick Children, London, England

WALT DISNEY'S
Peter Pan

r. and Mrs. Darling lived near a little park in Bloomsbury, a quiet part of London, with their three children, Wendy, John, and Michael. The children's nursemaid was a shaggy St. Bernard dog called Nana, who always knew exactly what medicine to give for a cough or a cold and could carry a spoon of the stuff in her mouth without spilling a drop. She was a treasure, Mrs. Darling often said.

At bedtime Wendy used to tell her younger brothers exciting stories about Never Land, a magical place where children remained young forever and had adventures with mermaids, Indians, pirates, fairies, and a remarkable boy named Peter Pan. "He has sometimes come to the foot of my bed and played on his pipes for me," Wendy confided to them. "The last time, Nana caught him at it and nipped off his shadow as he escaped."

One evening Mr. and Mrs. Darling were going out to a party. As they kissed the children good-night, Mr. Darling said to Wendy, "You're growing up, dear, and it's time you had a room of your own. This is your last night in the nursery." It so happened that on this same night the extraordinary adventures of the Darling children began.

A moment after Mr. and Mrs. Darling left the house, the nursery windows blew open and in flew Peter Pan and a fairy no larger than your hand. Her name was Tinker Bell and she moved in a sparkling shower of fairy dust. She flew about the room, searching for something, and finally landed in a dresser drawer full of sewing things. There, sure enough, was Peter Pan's lost shadow. Peter woke Wendy by playing on his pipes and asked her if she would be good enough to sew his shadow back to his feet again.

"I'm so glad you came tonight," Wendy told him as she sewed. "You see, I have to grow up tomorrow, and I might have missed you."

"I'll take you to Never Land with me. You'll *never* grow up there and you can tell stories to my Lost Boys every night," Peter said.

So they roused Michael and John out of their beds and, with a sprinkling of Tinker Bell's fairy dust, away they all flew, heading for Never Land, while Nana barked frantically down in the backyard.

Of all delightful islands, Never Land is the snuggest, with adventures all close together. The Lost Boys were looking for their leader, Peter Pan; the Indians were looking for the pirates; the pirates, led by the fierce Captain Hook, were after Peter, too. Peter had once, in a fair fight, cut off the Captain's hand, in place of which he now wore a hook. Worse yet, Peter had thrown the hand to a crocodile, who liked the taste so much that he had followed the Captain ever since in hope of getting the rest of him. Fortunately, the crocodile had also swallowed an alarm clock with a loud ticktock, which gave Hook fair warning when the creature was nearby. It was a sound that frightened the Captain out of his wits.

The Darling children looked down at their first glimpse of Never Land. "Oh, Peter," Wendy exclaimed, "it's just as I've dreamed it would be—Mermaid Lagoon, the Indian encampment—oh, and there's Captain Hook's pirate ship!" At that moment they heard the boom of a cannon from the ship, for Hook had seen Peter Pan in the sky. "Look out!" Peter yelled. "Tinker, take Wendy and the boys to the island. I'll stay up here and draw Hook's fire." But Tinker Bell was jealous of Wendy's friendship with Peter, and she purposely flew so fast that the children could not keep up with her.

Tinker zoomed down through the trees, to a hollow stump that was the entrance to the secret underground room where the Lost Boys lived. With the loveliest tinkle, as of golden bells (for that is the fairy language), she told the boys that Peter wanted them to attack the Wendy Bird and its brothers. When the children appeared, the boys pelted them with sticks and stones. Luckily, Peter Pan arrived just as the Lost Boys yelled "Hurray! We got the Wendy Bird!" He was very angry. "I bring you a mother to tell you stories and you knock her down," he scolded. And when Peter heard that it was Tinker's fault he sent her away for a week as punishment.

Then, Peter and Wendy flew off to Mermaid Lagoon while John and Michael joined the Lost Boys to fight the Indians. Wendy was enchanted by the mermaids' lovely lazy singing as they played in their lagoon. But Peter suddenly heard something in the distance. Leaping upon a rock that hung out over the sea he looked down and saw in a cove beneath him a boat from the pirate ship. "It's Hook!" he cried. At that dread name the mermaids plunged into the lagoon and disappeared. Captain Hook and his First Mate Smee had tied the Indian Princess Tiger Lily to a rock in the water. Peter and Wendy flew closer, but remained hidden.

"Now, me dear princess," said Hook, "you tell me the hiding place of Peter Pan and I'll set you free. Otherwise the tide will come in soon and you'll drown." Tiger Lily, however, bravely refused to betray her friend.

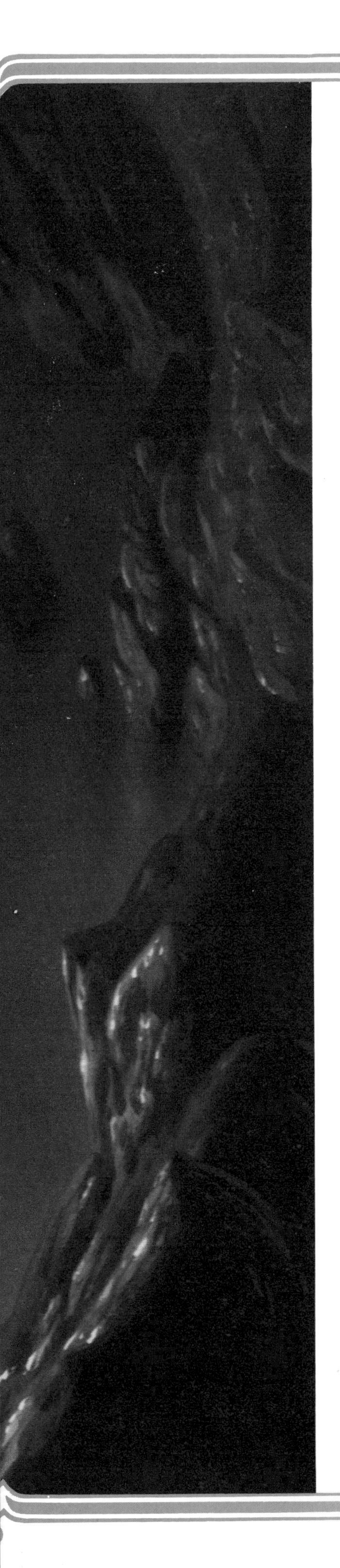

Peter tried to trick the two pirates into setting Tiger Lily free by imitating spirit voices. But Hook was suspicious and climbed up the rocky cliff with his sword drawn. When he saw Peter he shouted, "Hah! Pan, I'll get you for this!" Then he and Peter fought a fierce duel, to the very edge of the cliff. "I say, Captain, do you hear something?" Peter asked. There was a loud TICKTOCK, which so frightened the pirate he slipped and fell over the edge. There he hung by his hook, just above the hungry jaws of the crocodile.

Peter rescued Princess Tiger Lily in the nick of time, and he and Wendy flew with her to the Indian village where they all enjoyed a happy celebration with her father, the Chief. Meanwhile Smee saved his captain from the crocodile, who had already eaten Hook's trousers and was snapping his jaws for more.

Back at the pirate ship Captain Hook had the banished Tinker Bell brought to him. He slyly offered to sail away with Wendy who, he understood, had come between the little fairy and Peter. If Tinker would tell him how to find Peter's secret hiding place, where Wendy was living, Hook and the pirates would take the girl far away. Jealous little Tinker was delighted. She gave him the directions but added,

"You mustn't harm Peter!" The pirate assured her, "I won't lay a finger—or a hook—on Peter Pan." Then, laughing nastily he said, "Thank you, my dear," pushed Tinker Bell into a glass lantern, and shut it tight.

Gleefully the pirates listened to Captain Hook's instructions for finding Peter Pan's hideout and kidnapping him and all the others. They set out through the forest, found the entrance in the hollow tree, and hid themselves near it until the children came out. Below, in the hideaway, Wendy was tucking the Lost Boys into bed as she sang them a lullaby about home and mother. Instead of falling asleep, they all became so homesick that they decided to leave at once and return to their families. All except Peter Pan. "Go on!" he told them, "but I'm warning you. Once you're grown up you can never come back!" Wendy looked at him sadly and said, "I must go home to my mother and father. They'll miss us dreadfully." She followed the eager boys to the door. "Good-bye, Peter," she whispered.

As the children scrambled out of the hollow tree they were captured by the pirates and carried off, struggling, to the ship. Captain Hook and Smee remained behind with a gift for Peter—a package with a bomb inside. "I gave my word not to lay a finger, or a hook, on Peter Pan, and Captain Hook never breaks a promise. But when Pan opens this, it will blast him right out of Never Land!"

Aboard the ship the pirates told the children they must join the crew. "Unless you do," Hook threatened, "you'll walk the plank." "Oh, no, we won't," Wendy insisted. "Peter Pan will save us." Then Captain Hook told her of his little joke. "We left him a surprise package, you might say, that will explode as soon as he opens it. He won't be saving anyone, including himself."

When Tinker Bell, imprisoned in the lantern, heard those words she was sorry she had caused such terrible trouble for Peter and the children. Desperately she broke the lantern open and flew away to warn Peter.

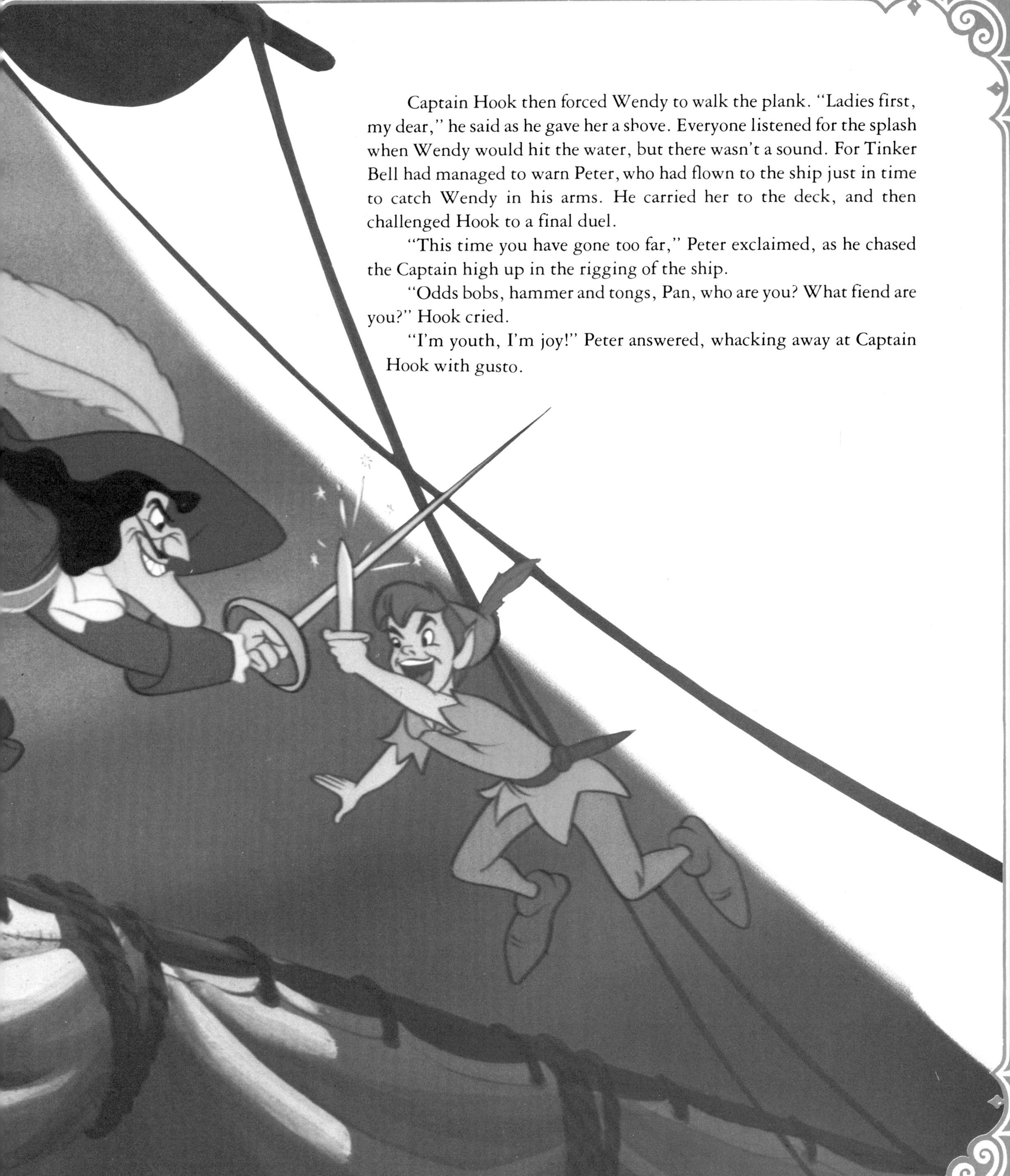

Captain Hook then forced Wendy to walk the plank. "Ladies first, my dear," he said as he gave her a shove. Everyone listened for the splash when Wendy would hit the water, but there wasn't a sound. For Tinker Bell had managed to warn Peter, who had flown to the ship just in time to catch Wendy in his arms. He carried her to the deck, and then challenged Hook to a final duel.

"This time you have gone too far," Peter exclaimed, as he chased the Captain high up in the rigging of the ship.

"Odds bobs, hammer and tongs, Pan, who are you? What fiend are you?" Hook cried.

"I'm youth, I'm joy!" Peter answered, whacking away at Captain Hook with gusto.

The boys chased the frightened pirates into their rowboat, and they rowed toward land as fast as they could, never once looking back. Hook took a tremendous swing at Peter, lost his footing, and plunged down into the sea below—where the crocodile waited. When last seen, the crocodile was chasing Hook, who was swimming after the pirates in the rowboat, who were rowing frantically for shore.

Now Peter Pan became captain of the ship. Tinker Bell, who was happy she had saved Peter and was his friend again, sprinkled the ship with fairy dust. The homesick boys hoisted the anchor and raised the sails, and the craft moved out to sea.

"Where are we sailing, Peter—I mean, Captain Pan?" Wendy asked.

"To London, madam," came the answer.

"Oh, Michael, John," Wendy called, "we're going home!"

At the nursery window Wendy, John, and Michael stood looking up at the starry sky. There, silhouetted against the pale moon, was what seemed to be a pirate ship under full sail, trailing fairy dust as it moved away into the distance. It had brought them safely back to the nursery, where the gangplank had been lowered through the open window. They had said good-bye to Tinker Bell and Peter Pan, and now they wanted to watch until the great ship sailed forever out of their sight.

Mr. and Mrs. Darling returned from their party and came up to the nursery with Nana.

"Oh, Mother," Wendy exclaimed, embracing Mrs. Darling, "we're back!"

"Back from where?" her mother asked.

"Never Land!" John and Michael shouted. "We came back on that ship way up in the sky." Mr. Darling looked out of the window where his children were pointing to something that appeared at first to be a cloud against the moon.

"You know," he said, "I have the strangest feeling that I've seen that ship before. A long time ago. When I was very young."

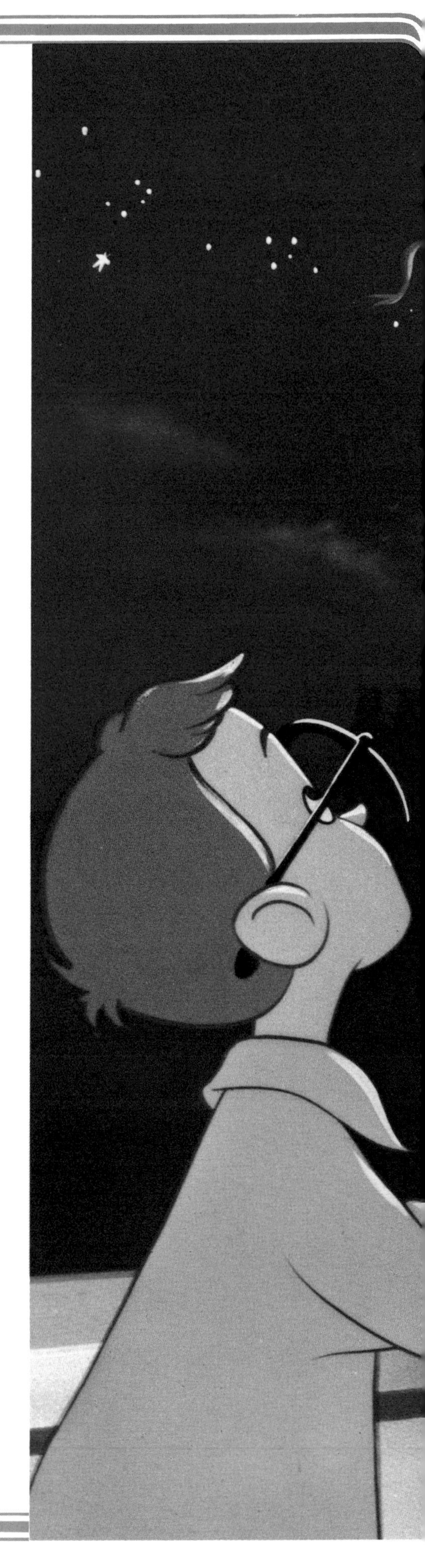

Kathryn Beaumont, whose voice and personality were used for the animated Wendy, watches layout artist Charles Phillipi make the first sketches

PETER PAN

The Story of the Production

The magical world of Peter Pan has never been so perfectly realized as in this animated feature. The landscape of Never Land, peopled by colorful and whimsical characters, was expanded to the furthest limits of fantasy by Walt Disney's imaginative genius. It was one of his most ambitious undertakings, in preparation for ten years and in active production for three more before its release in 1953.

During those thirteen years, every one of the Studio's top animators, background painters, and character developers worked on some aspect of the picture. More than nine hundred painted backgrounds were created, a record number at that time, and more than half a million drawings and sketches were made! The production cost $4 million, a much larger sum in 1953 than it is today.

Disney carefully read James M. Barrie's stage directions for the play *Peter Pan* as well as annotated scripts from later performances, which gave him many more clues for his production. When the animated feature was completed, he believed his screen version approximated what Barrie himself might have done had the technique of animation existed when his play was produced in 1904.

The role of Peter Pan has always been played by an actress, from the original Maude Adams to the more recent Mary Martin. Disney broke with that tradition and used the voice and personality of a real boy, Bobby Driscoll. The animators gave the cartoon character angular and manly gestures and action, in place of the more feminine tomboyishness that had become typical of Peter Pan, the boy who would not grow up.

Another unusual aspect of this picture for Disney is that most of the characters are people (Tinker Bell and the Mermaids have human forms), with the exception of Nana, the St. Bernard nursemaid, and the ticking crocodile that is Captain Hook's nemesis. It is the only Disney picture in which there are so few animal characters, and it illustrates the artists' greatly increased proficiency in animating the human body.

Youth, joy, and adventure come shining through this most beautiful version of a treasured classic, which, like its hero, refuses to grow old.

From Walt Disney's Motion Picture *Alice in Wonderland*, an adaptation of Lewis Carroll's *The Adventures of Alice in Wonderland* and *Through the Looking Glass*

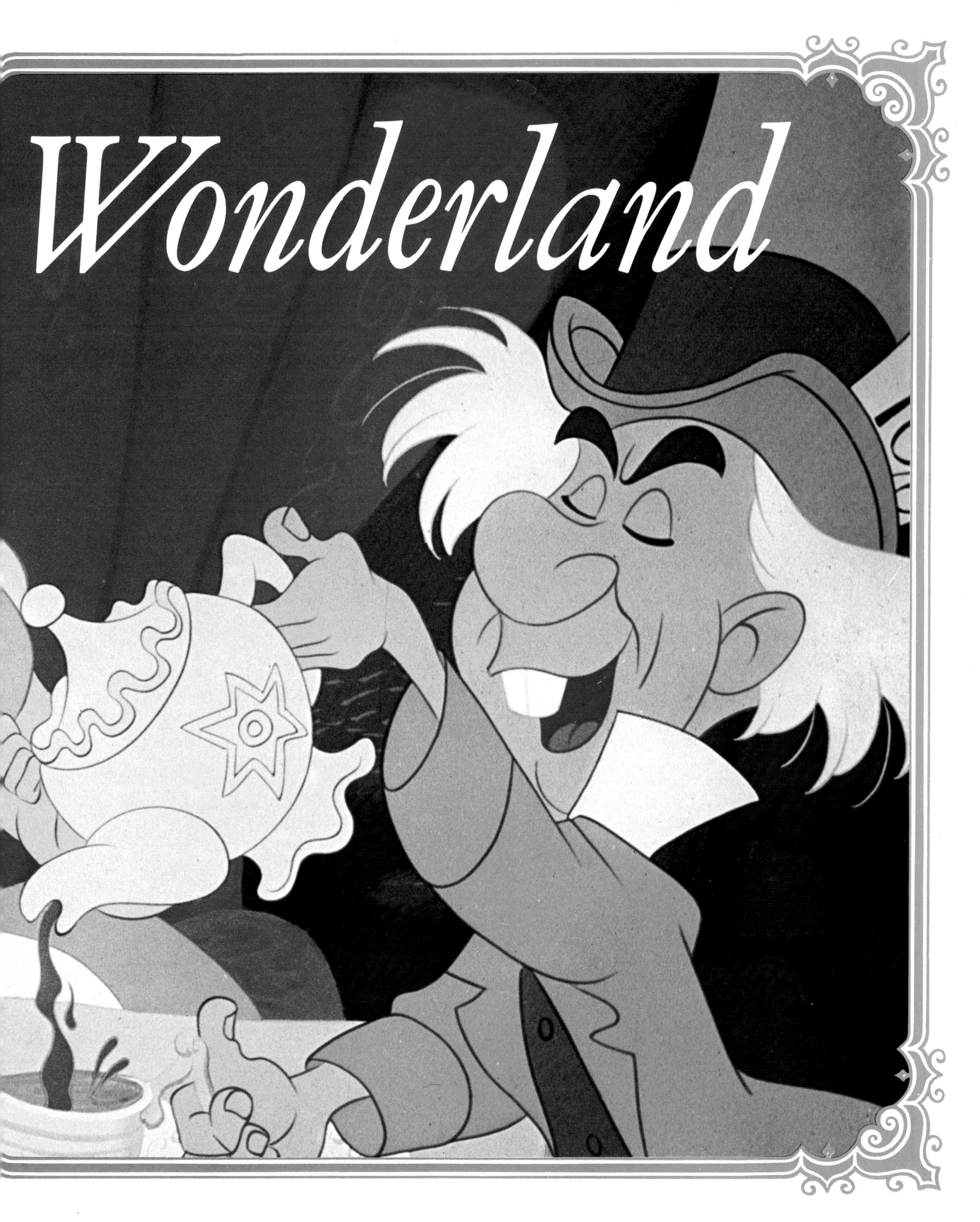
Wonderland

lice was beginning to get very tired of sitting by her sister on the riverbank and of having nothing to do. Once or twice she had peeped into the book her sister was reading, but it had no pictures or conversations in it. "And what is the use of a book," thought Alice, "without pictures or conversation?"

The hot day made her feel very sleepy, as she sat stroking her cat Dinah, when suddenly a White Rabbit with pink eyes ran close by her. Alice was not at all surprised to hear the Rabbit say, "Oh! my fur and whiskers, I'm late! I'm late! I'm late!" But when the Rabbit actually *took a watch out of its waistcoat pocket,* and looked at it, and then hurried on, Alice started to her feet. It flashed across her mind that she had never before seen a rabbit with either a waistcoat pocket or a watch to take out of it and, burning with curiosity, she ran after it just in time to see it pop down a large rabbit hole.

In another moment down went Alice after it, never once considering how in the world she was to get out again. The rabbit hole was very, very deep, but she fell very, very slowly and had plenty of time, as she went down, to look about her. The walls of the hole were lined with cupboards and shelves; here and there she saw maps and pictures hung on pegs. She took down a jar from one of the shelves as she passed. It was labeled "ORANGE MARMALADE," but to her great disappointment it was empty. Down, down, down—would the fall *never* come to an end? Suddenly, thump! thump! down she came upon a heap of sticks and dry leaves, and the fall was over.

Alice was not a bit hurt, and she jumped to her feet in a moment. Before her was another long passage; the White Rabbit was still in sight, hurrying down it. Away went Alice like the wind. She was close behind the Rabbit, but when she turned a corner, it was no longer to be seen.

Alice was in a long hall with doors all around it, but they were all locked. Behind a curtain, there was one small door, and when Alice peeked through its keyhole she saw a lovely garden. The Doorknob of this door startled Alice by speaking to her. "You're much too big to get through. Simply impassable." "You mean impossible," said Alice. "No," said the Doorknob. "Impassable. Nothing's impossible. Try the bottle on that table, next to the little gold key."

Alice took the bottle, which was labeled "DRINK ME," but the wise little girl was not going to do *that* in a hurry. She looked first to be sure it wasn't marked "*poison*." "For," Alice told herself, "if you drink much from a bottle marked '*poison*,' it's sure to disagree with you sooner

or later." This bottle had no such warning, so Alice drank it—and found herself growing smaller and smaller and smaller until she was only ten inches high. Just the right size for going through the door to the garden. But she had left the key on the table.

"Try the box," said the Doorknob. And Alice noticed a little box marked "EAT ME" on the floor. When she nibbled the cookie inside it, she immediately grew bigger and bigger until her head struck against the roof of the hall. "Curioser and curioser!" cried Alice. "Good-bye, feet!" When she stopped growing, she had become more than nine feet high. She at once took up the little golden key, but now, of course, she was much too big for the door to the garden.

Then Alice began to cry, and she cried and cried until there was a great pool of her tears. She saw the little bottle bobbing on the water and quickly drank the few drops remaining in it. Immediately she shrank to a tiny size and fell into the empty bottle. Riding safely within the bottle, Alice was swept on a wave of her own tears through the keyhole.

With the help of several strange creatures she encountered, Alice crawled out of the bottle and set off to explore the new land and to search for the White Rabbit. On her first adventure she met two fat, quarrelsome brothers, Tweedledee and Tweedledum, who insisted on reciting poems to her. First they did "The Walrus and the Carpenter," and Alice listened politely. When it was over she wanted to leave, but the Tweedle Twins insisted on another recitation, "Father William." While they were reciting the third verse, Alice quietly slipped away.

Soon she came upon a neat little house on the door of which was a bright brass plate with the name "W. RABBIT" engraved upon it. Just then the upstairs shutters flew open and the White Rabbit himself appeared. It called out, "Why, Mary Ann, what are you doing here? Run in this moment and fetch me my gloves."

The White Rabbit hurried out of the house, and waited impatiently while Alice searched inside for the gloves. She found a cookie jar labeled "TAKE ONE," so she did. Next thing she knew, Alice was growing again. She grew so huge that her arms and legs burst through the windows and doors, and she filled the little house until finally she split it apart. The White Rabbit, seeing the ruination of its home, cried out, "Help! Monster! There's a monster in my house!"

Its cries brought a Dodo and a lizard, both of whom tried to get Alice out of the house, but with no success. It was Alice herself who spied a carrot growing in the garden. "I wonder what will happen if I eat it," she thought and, reaching a giant hand out of the window, she picked it. As soon as she took a nibble she became small again. But by that time the White Rabbit had run off, muttering, "I'm late, I'm late. The Queen will be so angry! Oh no, can't wait, good-bye, hello, I'm late, I'm late, I'm late!"

Little Alice tried to follow the Rabbit through the garden, but it was too fast for her again. Noticing a cloud of smoke, Alice traced it to a large mushroom on which a caterpillar sat, contentedly blowing smoke rings as it puffed on its hookah. "Who are you?" the caterpillar demanded, when it saw the girl. "And exacticaly what is your problem?"

"Well," Alice answered, "it's exacticaly—I mean exactly—this: I should like to be a little larger, sir."

"Why?" the caterpillar demanded, blowing a beautiful question mark out of smoke.

"Well," said Alice, "three inches is such a wretched height."

The caterpillar, insulted at these words, said angrily, "*I* am exactly three inches high and it is a very good height indeed." And before Alice

UP
THIS WAY
DOWN
THIS WAY
YONDER
BACK
THAT WAY
GO BACK
THIS WAY

could apologize, the caterpillar had disappeared in a thick cloud of its own smoke. In its place a butterfly appeared. "By the way," the butterfly said, resuming the conversation (for, indeed, the caterpillar had changed into the butterfly), "I have another helpful hint for you: Eat one side of this mushroom and it will make you grow taller. And the other side will make you grow shorter." With that it flew away.

Alice nibbled from both sides of the mushroom until she had reached her normal size. "There," she sighed, "that's much better. I think I'll save these," and she pocketed two pieces of the magic mushroom, one from each side.

And now Alice found herself in a dark forest with no idea where to go to find the White Rabbit. The signs posted on the trees only added to her confusion. Looking about, she was startled to see a Cheshire Cat sitting on a bough of a tree grinning down at her. And since it had *very* long claws and a great many teeth, she felt it ought to be treated with respect.

"Cheshire Puss," she began timidly, "would you tell me please which way I ought to go from here?" "That depends on where you want to get to," said the Cat.

"I don't much care," Alice answered. "I'm looking for the White Rabbit."

"Well," said the Cat, "in *that* direction lives a Hatter and in *that* direction lives a March Hare. They're both mad."

Alice looked frightened. "We're all mad here," the Cat said. "I'm mad; you're mad or you wouldn't have come here." Then the Cheshire Cat began to vanish quite slowly, beginning with the end of its tail and ending with its grin, which remained some time after the rest of it had gone.

"Well, I've often seen a cat without a grin," thought Alice, "but a grin without a cat! It's the most curious thing I ever saw in all my life!"

Alice then decided to walk in the direction of the March Hare's house. A table was set out under a tree in front of the house, and the March Hare and the Hatter were having tea at it. A Dormouse was fast asleep between them and the other two were using it as a cushion, resting their elbows on it and talking over its head. They were having an unbirthday party. When they saw Alice coming they cried out, "No room! No room!"

"There's plenty of room," said Alice indignantly, sitting down in an armchair at one end of the table. It was the maddest tea party Alice had ever attended. What with changing seats and changing cups every few minutes, and the Hare and the Hatter trying to stuff the poor Dormouse into a teapot, and the conversation making no sense whatsoever, Alice was growing more and more bewildered. Abruptly the Hatter took his watch out of his pocket and asked, "What day of the month is it?" Alice thought a bit and then said, "The fourth."

"Two days slow," sighed the Hatter, shaking his watch and then holding it to his ear. "I told you butter wouldn't suit the works," he added, looking angrily at the March Hare.

"It was the *best* butter," the March Hare meekly replied. "Yes, but some crumbs must have got in as well," the Hatter grumbled. "You shouldn't have put it in with the bread-knife." Turning to Alice, he asked, "Do you think some tea might help it?"

"Really, now you ask me," said Alice, very much confused, "I don't think . . ."

"Then you shouldn't talk," said the Hatter.

This piece of rudeness was more than Alice could bear. She got up in great disgust and walked off. "I will find that White Rabbit," she thought angrily, "and ask him how to get home. I've had quite enough of this place."

Just then she noticed a little path between tall hedges. She followed it and soon found herself in a beautiful garden among bright flower beds and cool fountains. A large rose tree stood near the entrance of the

garden. The roses growing on it were white, but three playing-card gardeners were busily painting them red. When Alice asked them why, the Three of Clubs answered:

> We planted white roses by mistake,
> The Queen she likes them red.
> If she saw white—
> She'd raise a fuss,
> And each of us
> Would quickly lose his head.

At this moment the Two of Clubs called out, "The Queen! The Queen!" The three gardeners immediately threw themselves flat on their faces. There was a sound of many footsteps and Alice looked round, eager to see the Queen. Soldiers and courtiers, among them the White Rabbit, formed a grand procession, and last of all came the King and Queen of Hearts.

When they reached Alice, the Queen said severely, "Who is this?" No one answered. "Idiots!" said the Queen, tossing her head impatiently. "What's your name, child? Look up. Speak nicely." Alice curtsied and replied politely. "But," she thought, "they're only a pack of cards after all. I needn't be afraid of *them*."

So when the Queen demanded to know who were the three cards lying on their faces, Alice, surprised at her own courage, answered, "How should *I* know? It's no business of *mine*."

The Queen turned crimson with fury. "Off with her head!" she screamed.

"Nonsense," said Alice very loudly and decidedly, and the Queen was silent.

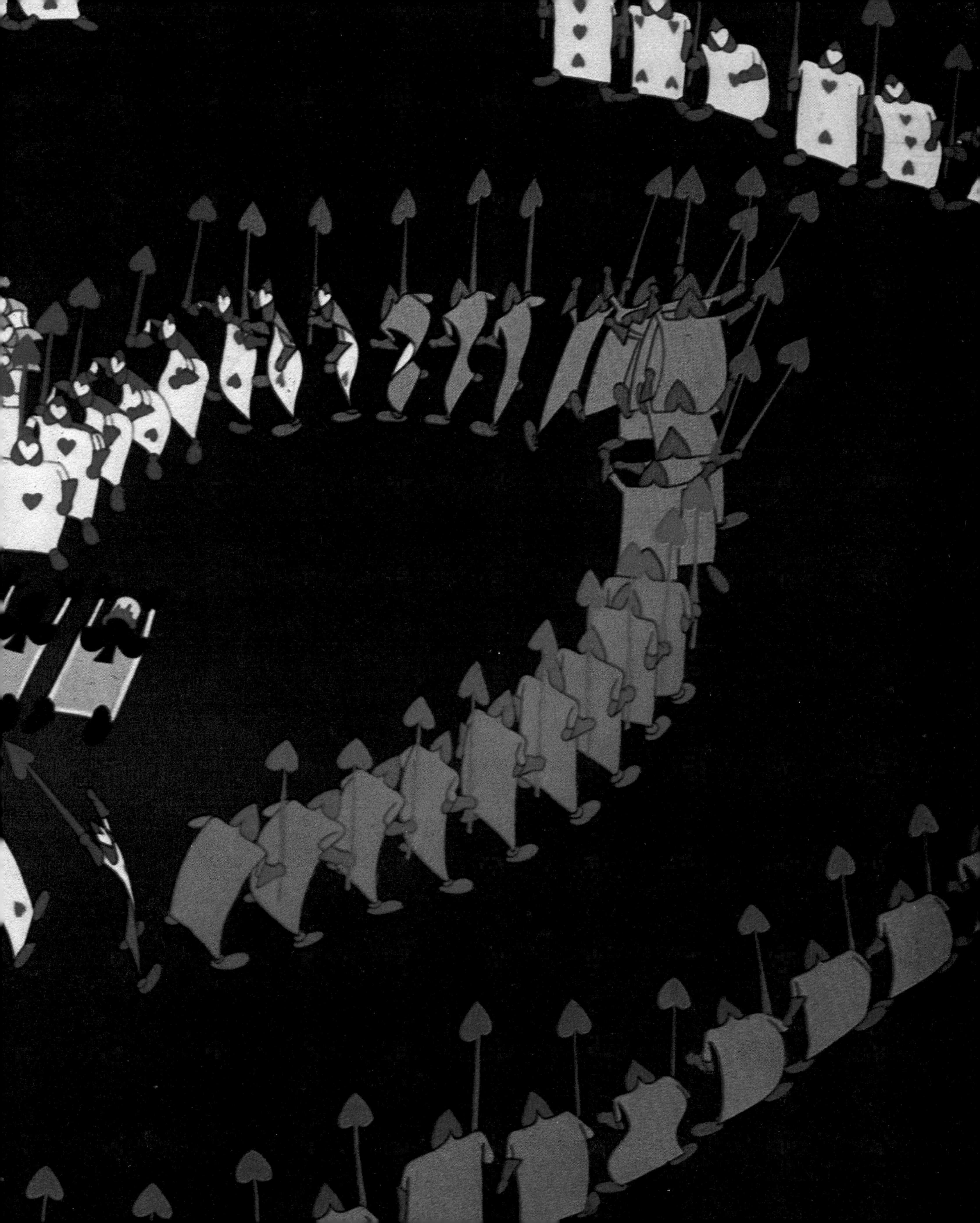

"Can you play croquet?" shouted the Queen. "Yes!" shouted Alice. "Come on, then," roared the Queen.

Alice was given a flamingo for a mallet and a hedgehog for a ball. The players all played at once without waiting for their turns, quarreling and fighting, while the Queen went about stamping and shouting "Off with his head!" or "Off with her head!" In the midst of the turmoil the Cheshire Cat appeared. Then it disappeared, and appeared again somewhere else. The Queen was provoked by its pranks and, since Alice talked to the Cat and seemed to be its friend, the Queen demanded that she be put on trial.

Alice was then put in the prisoner's dock, where she became truly alarmed about what might happen to her. The White Rabbit—late as ever—read the charges. Then the Queen banged her fist on the bench and shouted, "Sentence first, verdict afterward! Off with her head!" Alice, really frightened, put her hand in her apron pocket and felt something there. It was the mushroom. She popped both pieces in her mouth, one after the other. Suddenly she grew to her full size, and the tiny cards jabbing her ankles were nothing to fear.. Alice picked up a handful and flipped them away. "Why, you're nothing but a pack of cards," she said.

At this the whole pack rose up into the air and came flying down upon her. Alice gave a little scream and tried to beat them off—she found herself lying beneath a tree on the riverbank with Dinah in her lap. Some leaves were fluttering down upon her face.

"Wake up, Alice dear," said her sister. "What a long sleep you've had!"

"Oh, I've had such a curious dream," said Alice, "a dream of Wonderland."

"Well now, run in for your tea; it's getting late."

So Alice got up and ran off, thinking what a wonderful dream it had been, all on a happy summer day.

ALICE IN WONDERLAND

The Story of the Production

On a "golden afternoon" in 1862—July 4th to be exact—Charles Lutwidge Dodgson, an Oxford mathematics don, took three little sisters boating on the Isis. The middle sister, ten-year-old Alice Liddell, asked for a story from the young man, one "with plenty of nonsense in it," to while away the time. Wishing to please the child he started with these words: "Alice was beginning to get very tired of sitting by her sister. . . ." And thus one of the great classics in the English language was born. "The interminable fairy tale," as Dodgson called it, went on for many future meetings. Eventually the author hand-lettered the whole story, drew thirty-seven illustrations for it, and presented the charming manuscript book to Alice Liddell for Christmas in 1864. He titled it *Alice's Adventures under Ground.*

Revised and expanded, the book was published on July 4, 1865, the third anniversary of the boating party. John Tenniel drew the illustrations, some of them not unlike the author's; the title became *Alice's Adventures in Wonderland;* and the author signed himself Lewis Carroll—all three names were destined for worldwide fame.

In 1949, Walt Disney chose Alice's fantastic adventures as an ideal vehicle for animation. For nearly two years he and a staff of 750 artists worked on the production, transposing Carroll's text and Tenniel's illustrations to their medium as faithfully as possible.

During a story conference on *Alice in Wonderland,* Winston Hibler, Ted Sears, Walt Disney, and Ed Penner review sketches and storyboards

Alice in the recording studio—Jerry Colonna, Kathryn Beaumont, and Ed Wynn create the sound track for the March Hare's and Mad Hatter's tea party

For the voices of the zany characters that Alice meets in Wonderland, a cast of highly idiosyncratic comedians was assembled: Ed Wynn's giddy giggle became the Mad Hatter's; Jerry Colonna's vocal eccentricities helped to delineate the March Hare; the Cheshire Cat's voice was Sterling Holloway's; Richard Haydn's supercilious tones made the Caterpillar a standout. Verna Felton spoke commandingly for the terrible-tempered Queen of Hearts. J. Pat O'Malley, a man with many vocal talents, provided voices for Tweedledee and Tweedledum, the Walrus, the Carpenter, and the Oysters. A British actress, Kathryn Beaumont, supplied Alice's girlish voice, as she was later to do for Wendy in *Peter Pan*.

Alice in Wonderland was a musical, and among its best songs were "I'm Late," "Alice in Wonderland," "All in a Golden Afternoon," "Unbirthday Song," and "Very Good Advice."

With this feature, released in 1951, Walt Disney succeeded in bringing Alice to the screen in a form which pleased both the traditionalists and the large new audience not previously acquainted with her and her curious companions.

From Walt Disney's Motion Picture *Bambi,* adapted from the story by Felix Salten. The edition containing the full text of *Bambi, a Life in the Woods* by Felix Salten is published in the U. S. by Simon & Schuster and in the United Kingdom by Jonathan Cape Limited

Bambi

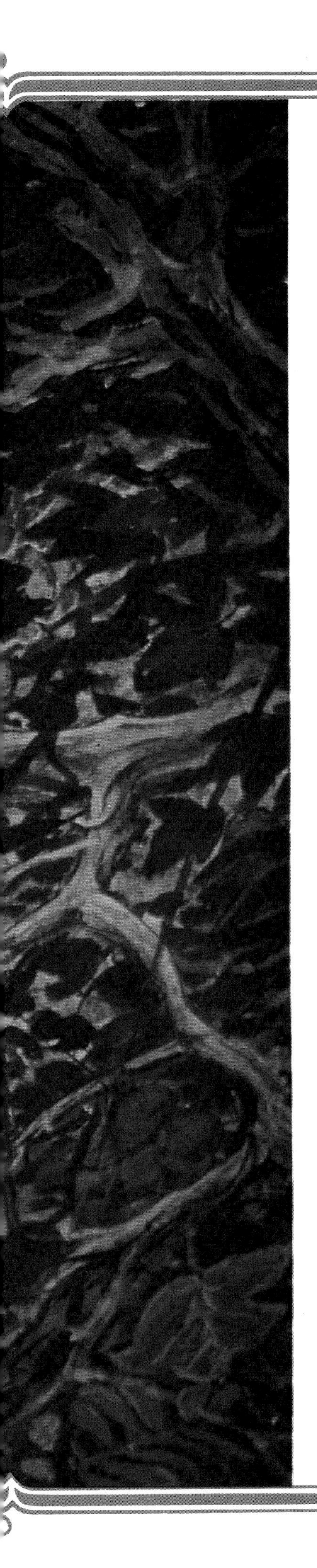

e came into the world early one morning, in the middle of a little forest glade screened in by leaves and branches on all sides. There was barely room for him and his mother. The baby fawn stood swaying on wobbly legs, as if surprised to find himself out in the strange world.

"What a beautiful child," said a magpie, perching on a nearby branch. "How remarkable that he can stand up by himself after just being born!" Her chirping and chattering aroused the other forest creatures, who hurried to the thicket to admire the new baby. "It isn't every day," said the owl, "that a Prince of the Forest is born. Congratulations."

The mother didn't answer because she was busy washing the fawn, licking him gently with her warm tongue. His little red coat with fine white spots was still somewhat mussed, and on his baby face there was still a deep, dreamy expression. The fawn sank down and snuggled sleepily against his mother, hunting eagerly until he found nourishment for his life. While he suckled, his mother continued her warm caresses. "Bambi," she whispered. "My little Bambi."

By early summer Bambi was frisking along behind his mother as she walked the narrow paths that ran through the woods. Wild flowers twinkled like white, yellow, and purple stars among the green leaves. The voices of a thousand woodland creatures murmured and buzzed and hummed. And one creature, a little bunny named Thumper, thumped.

"Good morning, Prince Bambi," someone called from overhead. Bambi turned his head upside down, and there, to his astonishment, he saw a family of opossums hanging from a branch by their long thin tails. The next thing he knew, he tripped over a rock and went sprawling.

His mother turned back and licked him comfortingly. Thumper hopped over and said, "Come on, Bambi. Get up, and try again." When Bambi stood up on his spindle-legs, Thumper and his sister frolicked around him. Thumper thumped on a log with his hind legs. "I'm thumpin'," he announced. "That's why they call me Thumper." Bambi looked at him admiringly, but said not a word.

A family of birds flew past and alighted on the branches of a tree where they warbled their little song. Bambi looked at them curiously. "Those are birds," Thumper told him. "Say 'bird,' Bambi." "Bur, Bur," said Bambi. The rabbits hopped about excitedly. The young Prince had spoken his first word! Bambi was so pleased with himself he kept saying "Bur. Bur. Bur," until suddenly he said it right, "BIRD!"

Just then a butterfly flew into the clearing and settled down right on Bambi's tail. Bambi spun round to look at it. "Bird," he said. "No, Bambi, that's a butterfly," Thumper explained. Bambi leapt toward a bush of bright flowers that resembled the butterfly. "Butterfly!" he said proudly. "No," Thumper corrected him again. "That's a flower," and he bent down to smell a blossom. Bambi, too, put his head down to smell the flower, but found himself face to face with a small skunk, who had hidden behind the bush. "Flower!" he exclaimed. "No," said Thumper, rolling on the ground with laughter. "That's no flower, that's a skunk!" The skunk, however, liked his new name. "The Prince can call me Flower if he wants to," he said. "I don't mind."

There was a sudden flash of lightning and the rumble of thunder in the distance. "I think I'd better go home now," said Thumper. "It's going to rain." And off he ran. Bambi had no idea what "rain" meant, but the loud noise frightened him and he ran to find his mother. They both made their way to the thicket, where they lay down to sleep. But Bambi was soon awakened by the splashing sound of water, the fresh, wet, earthy smell, and the plop of a raindrop that now and then landed on the tip of his nose. So this was rain! The lightning flashed again and the thunder boomed closer. Bambi snuggled nearer to his mother. She bent her head over, covering him and shutting out the noise and the wet. Very soon Bambi fell back to sleep.

One morning Bambi followed his mother out of the forest and into the big open meadow. "We must be careful here," she warned. "There are no trees and bushes to hide us, so we must be sure it's safe." She stopped at the edge of the wide open space and stood motionless as she sniffed the wind, looked in all directions, and, with head held high, listened intently. At last, she said, "Come on, Bambi, it's all right."

There were other deer out in the meadow, nibbling at the sweet clover. And there was a pond with a duck and a frog. Bambi's eyes grew larger and larger as they surveyed this broad new world. He drew back, startled, when a strange fawn bounded over to him. He had never seen one before. The fawn, trying to be friendly, edged closer to Bambi. He backed away, stumbled over a root, turned and dashed off to his mother. The strange fawn followed. Bambi's mother looked down at him, amused at his shyness. "That's little Faline," she said, "your Aunt Ena's daughter. Run along and play with her."

Bambi turned slowly toward Faline. Suddenly she gave a leap and rushed away. In a moment Bambi darted after her. They ran in a broad circle, they leapt into the air three, four, five times. Bambi had never felt so wildly happy. The sweet smell of the meadow, the open sky, the warmth of the sun made him leap for joy.

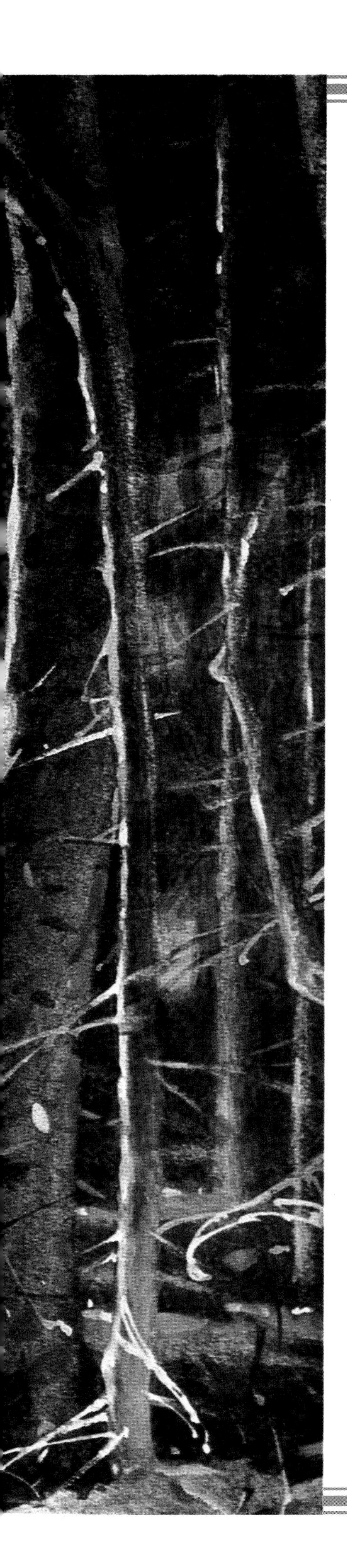

Then something happened that was more exciting than anything else that had happened to Bambi that day. Out of the forest came the sound of hoofs beating on the ground. Branches snapped and someone burst out of the thicket. He looked like Bambi's mother but was larger, and his head was crowned with gleaming antlers. He was stately and noble, his head held royally high and his splendid antlers rising above it. Bambi was overcome with admiration. In the hush that fell over the meadow the stately stag passed by in silent splendor. The fawns didn't dare to breathe until he had disappeared into the thicket.

"Who was that?" Bambi whispered to his mother. "That was your father," she said. "Of all the deer in the forest he is the bravest and wisest. That's why he's known as the Great Prince of the Forest."

"How handsome he is," Bambi sighed. His mother smiled down at him. "If you are cunning, my son, and don't run into danger, you'll be as strong and handsome as your father someday, and you'll have antlers like his, too."

Time passed; the leaves fell from the trees and the cold winds blew through the forest. One morning Bambi awoke in the little thicket next to his mother to find that the world had changed overnight. It smelled different, and when Bambi peered out, the trees and bushes were covered with whiteness. "Mother, look," he cried. "What is that white stuff?" "That's snow," she answered. "Winter has come."

At first it was fun to play with Thumper and Faline and his other friends in the soft white snow. But then Bambi noticed that life had become much harsher. Before, they had all lived a rich life with plenty to eat in meadow and forest, and Bambi, who had known only abundance, thought he would always have plenty to eat. But now it grew harder and harder to find food. Bambi had to dig the snow away with his little hoof to find one withered blade of grass. The icy crust cut his delicate legs.

Bambi's mother taught him how to feed on the bark of a tree. She could stand on her hind legs and reach up high to rip a piece of bark off for him to share. But as winter wore on, the trees were stripped of their bark by hungry deer, and there was less and less to eat. "Winter sure is long, isn't it?" Bambi complained. "It seems long, but it won't last forever," his mother assured him. "I'm *so* hungry," Bambi sighed.

So, although the meadow was dangerous except in the evening or early morning, Bambi's mother took him there one afternoon. Pawing aside the snow, she called, "Look here. Grass, new spring grass!" Lowering their heads, the two deer ate hungrily, two dark shapes alone in the middle of the great white meadow.

All at once they heard the magpies warning, "Look out! Look out!"

Bambi and his mother raised their heads and sniffed the air. And there it was, a heavy wave of scent that meant Man. At the same moment they heard the crash of a gunshot. "Run, Bambi. Don't look back—keep running no matter what, to the thicket," and Bambi's mother was off with a bound that barely skimmed the snow.

The thunder of Man's guns was all about, and then the sounds grew fainter as Bambi ran deeper into the forest. Outside their thicket he waited for his mother, calling her as he wandered through the trees. "Mother! Mother!" There was no answer.

Bambi's eyes widened in astonishment when out of the winter twilight the Great Stag appeared. "Your mother can't be with you anymore," he said in his stern but gentle voice. "Now you must be brave and learn to walk alone. Come, my son," he added as he turned and moved off through the trees. There was nothing for Bambi to do but to follow.

Time passed and it was spring, when all the forest animals fall in love, or as the owl put it, "become twitterpated." They had all grown during the winter, and his friends almost didn't recognize Bambi, who had traded in his spots for a pair of small antlers. Flower the skunk was the first of the group to fall in love. He saw a pair of mischievous blue eyes peeking out of a clump of black-eyed Susans. There was a soft giggle, and the blue eyes winked. Then a little girl skunk emerged and kissed Flower. From that moment on, Flower followed her about, completely "twitterpated."

Thumper was next, losing his heart to a honey-colored bunny. Bambi vowed such foolishness was not for him, but when he saw his old playmate Faline, now a beautiful young doe with a soft tan coat and large brown eyes, he became as "twitterpated" as any creature in the forest.

"Will you stay with me, Faline?" he asked her. Faline moved toward Bambi and was about to answer when a rival buck named Ronno moved roughly between Faline and Bambi. Shaking his antlers and pawing the ground, he dared Bambi to take one step closer to the doe. Bambi, enraged, charged at the buck, and they fought, antler to antler, while Faline watched and wished very hard that Bambi would win. Pushing and straining, Bambi finally braced with his hind legs and hurled himself at Ronno. The buck fell to the ground, while Bambi stood over him, victorious. Then he led Faline away. "You were wonderful," she said softly. All that summer they were together.

Once again the autumn winds were blowing. Bambi awoke one morning and sensed that something was wrong. Leaving Faline in their thicket, the young buck explored the forest, searching for the danger.

At the edge of a cliff he was joined by the Great Stag. They looked down into the valley in the early morning mist, and saw a campfire and movement. And smelled that fearsome smell. "Man," said the Stag in his deep voice. "There are many this time. More than I have ever seen before." The crows flew off to caw their warning. "Quickly," the Stag commanded. "To the hills!"

Bambi went to join Faline, but she had left their thicket in search of him. Each called through the forest to the other. "Bambi!" "Faline!" Meanwhile pheasants, quail, rabbits, birds, and every animal large and small hurried to make their escape from Man. Shots rang through the forest.

Then a pack of savage hunting dogs raced through the woods. They were chasing Faline. The doe bounded away, her heart pounding as the dogs snarled at her heels. She leapt up to a rocky ledge, and turned to see the dogs scrambling below her and barking loudly. She was cornered and could go no further. "Bambi!" she called.

Bambi had heard the barking and when he recognized Faline's call

he came running. He charged the pack of dogs and then reared up on his hind legs, using his sharp front hoofs to slash at any dogs who attacked. They kept a respectful distance. "Jump, Faline," he called to her, "and run home." When he thought Faline was safe, Bambi turned and ran at top speed, once even leaping over a fallen tree. There was an unexpected crash of sound and at the same moment a sharp pain in his leg. Bambi stumbled and fell, wounded by a gunshot.

He had not lain there long when squirrels, rabbits, and other small animals ran past him. "Get up, Bambi! Get up! The forest is on fire!" they cried as they fled toward the stream to safety. And then, as smoke began to drift into that part of the forest, the Great Stag appeared. "Get up, Bambi," he ordered. Bambi struggled to rise and the Stag encouraged him. "Get up, Bambi. You can," he said. "Now, follow me."

As Bambi limped behind the Stag, the smoke stung his eyes and every now and then a flash of flame jumped from one tree to another. "Man caused this, too, with a little cinder from his campfire," said the Stag. "We must follow the stream to the island. The fire can't reach us

there." They both plodded through the water, with hundreds of other creatures around them. At the tip of the island various small animals huddled, and in the tree branches families of birds stared across the river as their forest home was destroyed. Bambi was in despair when out of the gloom he heard his name called as only one creature in the whole world could call him. "Faline!" he responded joyfully. The two were reunited at the water's edge and they stood, shoulder to shoulder, watching the terrible spectacle in silence.

Another spring came, flowers bloomed once again, tender green leaves sprouted on live trees, covering the charred remains of the fire. Flower and Owl and Thumper had families, and they all were hurrying to the thicket to see Faline and her twin fawns.

Bambi and the Great Stag looked on from a distance. "Don't follow me any further, Bambi," said the Great Stag in a calm voice. "My time is up and I must look for a resting place. Good-bye, my son. I loved you dearly." Soundlessly he disappeared into the bushes without stirring a leaf.

Bambi was now the Great Prince of the Forest.

BAMBI

The Story of the Production

When Walt Disney read Felix Salten's *Bambi, a Life in the Woods* in 1937 (the year that *Snow White* was released) he knew at once that he wanted to make an animated feature based on the book. The story of a deer's life from birth to maturity was written with great feeling and tenderness by the well-known Austrian author.

In order to capture the beauty and sensitivity of the book, Disney realized that a great deal of careful naturalistic detail would be required. During the three years of planning before animation was begun, he sent artist Maurice Day on a five-month trip to the Maine woods to photograph and sketch animals, bushes, trees, cloud formations, bark patterns, snowdrifts, and fire-ravaged forests. Other artists were sent to western woodlands. Back at the Studio, an imaginary forest setting was charted and mapped so that each animator would have a guide for the position of every tree and rock in his background scenes.

The multiplane camera, which gives depth of detail from foreground to background, was used extensively in filming *Bambi,* with as many as nine separate levels being photographed at one time. The scenic artists who painted the forest scenes worked in oils rather than the customary tempera to achieve greater richness of detail and perspective.

Although animals like Thumper the rabbit, Flower the skunk, and the wise owl are amusing cartoon characters, the deer and other forest creatures are rendered with greater fidelity to nature. Two live fawns, two skunks, some squirrels, birds, rabbits, chipmunks, and other denizens of the forest were kept in an animal compound at the Disney Studio in Burbank during the entire production time. They served as living models for the animators, who attended special art classes in drawing animals and their movements.

Bambi was released in 1942, five years after it was first planned. It is unique among Disney's animated features for its poetic naturalism and scenic grandeur.

A life class for the Disney artists brought the woodland creatures right into the Studio

Peter Behn, the voice of Thumper, feeds the rabbit model while animators Ollie Johnston, Milt Kahl, and Frank Thomas look on

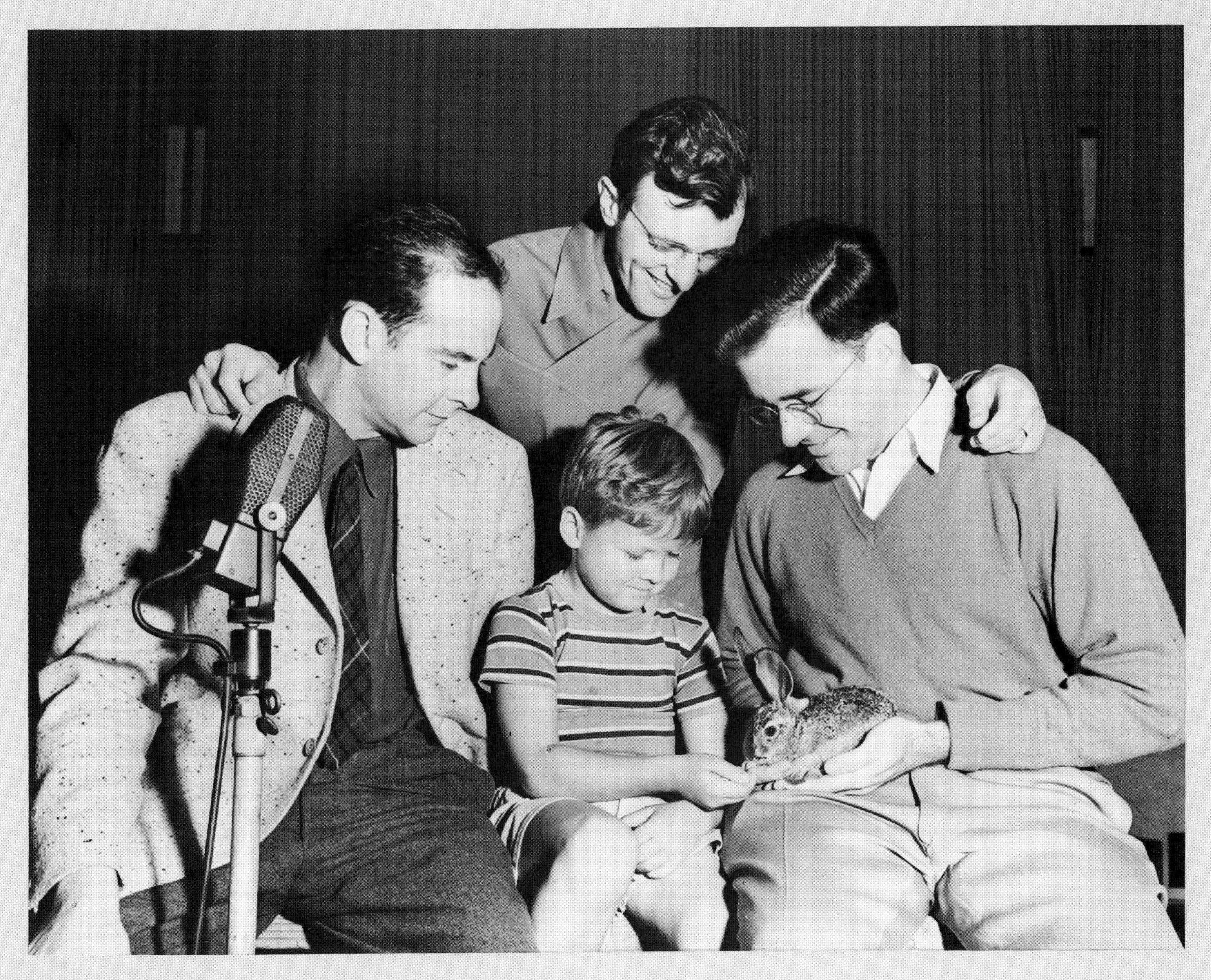

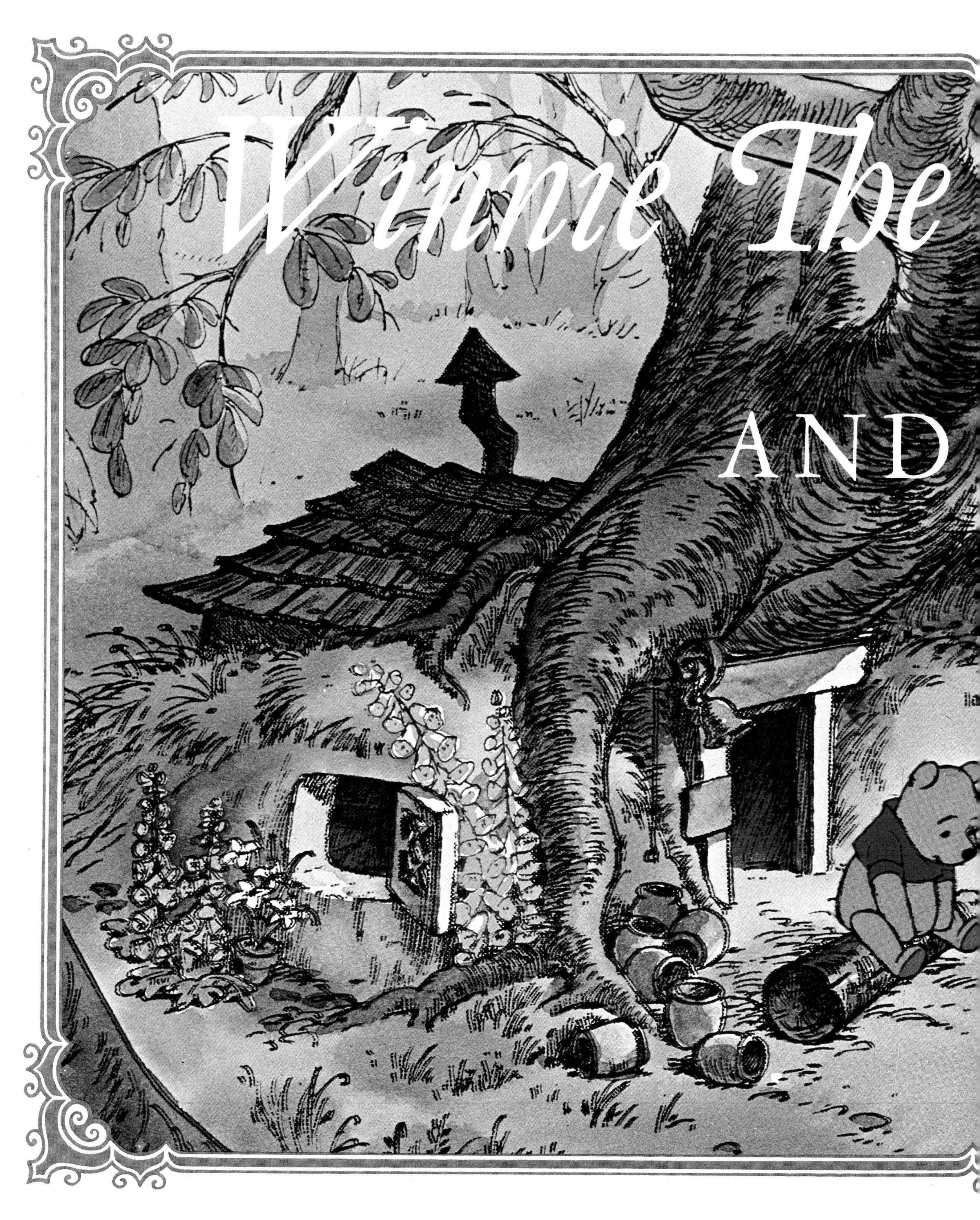
Winnie The
AND

Pooh
The Honey
Tree
From Walt Disney's Motion Picture *Winnie the Pooh and the Honey Tree,* based on the books by A. A. Milne, published in the United States by E. P. Dutton & Co. Inc. and in the United Kingdom by Methuen and Company, Ltd.

MR SANDERZ
RNIG ALSO
HUNN

Like most small boys, Christopher Robin had toy animals to play with, and they all lived together in a wonderful world of make-believe.

His best friend was a bear called Winnie the Pooh, or Pooh for short. Now Pooh had some very unusual adventures, and they all happened deep in the Hundred Acre Wood, where Christopher Robin played. It was the enchanted neighborhood of Christopher Robin's childhood.

Winnie the Pooh lived in the Hundred Acre Wood all by himself under the name of Sanders, which means he had the name over the door in gold letters and he lived under it.

One day when Pooh was sitting by the fire warming his hands, he heard his clock strike. When he heard that sound, he knew it was time for something, but what could it be? Since he was a bear of very little brain, he had to think about it in the most thoughtful way he could.

"Oh yes!" he said at last, getting to his feet. "Time for my Stoutness Exercises." And he stood before his mirror and began to touch his toes and straighten up while he sang a little song:

When I up-down,
Touch-the-ground,
It puts me in the mood,
Up-down, touch-the-ground,
In the mood for food.
I am stout, round,
And I have found,
Speaking poundage-wise,
I improve my appetite
When I exercise.

After finishing his exercises Pooh wondered what to do next. It was about eleven o'clock in the morning, just the time for something sweet, so he went to his cupboard and took down a jar of honey. But the jar was empty.

"Oh bother," said Pooh. "There's only a little left." And he pushed his face deep into the honey pot so he could lick the last bit.

While he had the honey pot over his face, a bee flew in the window and buzzed past Pooh's ear. "That buzzing noise means something," said the bear. "The only reason for making a buzzing noise, that *I* know of, is because you're a bee!" He pulled the pot off his face and watched

the bee fly out the window. "And the only reason for being a bee is to make honey." Pooh followed the bee outdoors and watched it fly into a hole in a nearby tree. "And the only reason for making honey is so *I* can eat it!"

Eagerly, Pooh headed for the tree and started to climb. He climbed and he climbed and he climbed, and as he climbed he hummed a little hum to cheer himself up. The climb was getting harder and harder and Pooh was swinging dangerously on a very thin branch. *Crack!*

"Oh, help!" said Pooh, as he dropped to the branch below.

"If only I hadn't—you see, what I meant to do-oo!" he said, bumping from branch to branch.

"It all comes, I suppose, from," he sighed as he flew gracefully into a prickly bush, "from *liking* honey so much. Oof! Oh bother!"

He crawled out of the bush, brushed the prickles from his nose, and sat down to think again. And the first person he thought of was Christopher Robin.

So Winnie the Pooh went to see his friend Christopher Robin, who lived in a tree trunk in another part of the forest where he could be near his friends and help them.

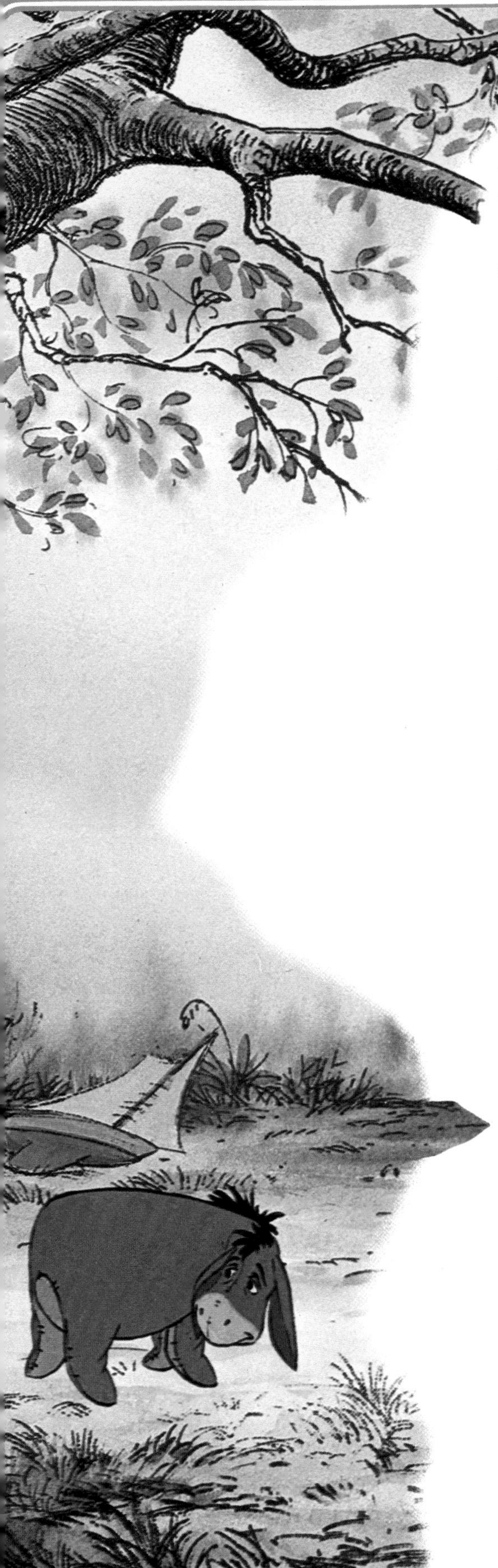

Christopher had just finished nailing on Eeyore's tail. The donkey, who was forever losing his tail, looked at it gloomily. "Thanks," he said. "It's not much of a tail, but I'm sort of attached to it."

Just then Pooh arrived. "Good morning, Christopher Robin," he called.

"Good morning, Winnie the Pooh," said Christopher Robin.

"If it is a good morning," said Eeyore, "which I doubt." And he jogged off.

Pooh looked at the toys in front of Christopher's house. "I just said to myself coming along: 'I wonder if Christopher Robin has such a thing as a balloon about him?' I just said it to myself, while thinking of balloons and wondering."

"What do you want a balloon for?" asked Christopher, as he untied a blue balloon.

Winnie the Pooh looked carefully in all directions to be sure that no one was listening. Then he put his paw near his mouth, and growled in a deep whisper, *"Honey!"*

"But you don't get honey with a balloon!"

"I do," said Pooh.

"How?" asked Christopher, handing him the string of the balloon.

"I shall fly like a bee, up to the honey tree, see?" And Pooh floated up in the air with the balloon.

Christopher caught him just in time. "Oh, Pooh, you can't fool the bees that way."

"Wait and see," said Pooh.

He went to a very muddy place that he knew of, and rolled and rolled in the mud until he was black all over. "Now," he explained, "I'll be a little black rain cloud under the sky-blue balloon."

Christopher Robin smiled at Pooh affectionately. "Silly old bear," he said.

They walked over to the honey tree together, Pooh holding on to the balloon and Christopher Robin holding on to Pooh. Pooh pointed up at the hole and asked Christopher to aim him at the bees. Christopher gave the bear a little lift in the right direction, let go suddenly, and there was Pooh Bear, floating gracefully up into the sky, level with the bees' nest, but about twenty feet away from it.

"Hooray!" Christopher Robin shouted.

"How do I look?" Pooh called down.

"You look like a chubby bear holding on to the string of a balloon," said Christopher. "Careful, Pooh. Hold on tight!"

"I'm only a little black rain cloud," Pooh sang. "Pay no attention to little me."

Pooh Bear floated closer to the hole and reached a paw in for some honey. A bee flew out and buzzed around his nose.

"Christopher Robin," Pooh called, "I think the bees s-u-s-p-e-c-t something. Go home and get your umbrella and walk around saying, 'Tut-tut, it looks like rain.' I think it would help fool the bees."

Christopher returned with his umbrella and Pooh sang a little Cloud Song, such as a rain cloud might sing. But the bees were buzzing more suspiciously than ever. Some flew out of their nest and gathered round and round the cloud as it began the second verse of its song. One bee even sat down on the cloud's nose.

Then a swarm of angry bees attacked the balloon. It began to lose air and Winnie the Pooh floated slowly down toward the ground.

"Christopher Robin!!" Pooh called. "Oh bother! I think I shall come down." But Christopher caught him before he could hit the ground. Using the umbrella as a shield they splashed across a mud pond, leaving the angry bees behind.

"I've been thinking, Christopher Robin," said Pooh, as they sloshed across the pond. "And I have come to a very important decision. Christopher Robin, *you never can tell with bees.*"

WINNIE THE POOH AND THE HONEY TREE

The Story of the Production

In 1966, Walt Disney released the first animated featurette based on A. A. Milne's children's classic, *Winnie-the-Pooh.* Running a little under half an hour, the film version of this enchanting adventure of a small boy, Christopher Robin, and his favorite toy bear, Winnie the Pooh, has been seen by millions of new fans in theaters and on television. In bringing Milne's characters to life through animation, Disney and his creative staff remained faithful to Ernest H. Shepard's original book illustrations, themselves almost as famous and beloved as the stories.

A. A. Milne, an English novelist and playwright, wrote a book of verse about his four-year-old son in 1924, *When We Were Very Young.* This was followed by a second book of verse, *Now We Are Six,* and by two volumes of stories about Christopher Robin and his toy animals, *Winnie-the-Pooh* and *The House at Pooh Corner.* Christopher and his stuffed toys all lived in a delightful woodland, very much like that surrounding Milne's country house in Sussex. Shepard, a friend and neighbor, captured the characters and setting with inspired authenticity in his drawings for all four books. The books have been translated into twelve languages and have sold close to fifteen million copies.

At the Walt Disney Studio in Burbank, an actor dressed as Winnie the Pooh cavorts in front of the Animation Building

John Lounsbery, one of Disney's veteran animators, brings Eeyore, the dolorous donkey, to life

Wolfgang (Woolie) Reitherman, the director of the film, also directed Disney's *The Sword in the Stone, The Jungle Book, Robin Hood,* and *The Aristocats.* Working closely with Reitherman on the animation were eleven of Disney's veteran artists, including Hal King, John Lounsbery, John Sibley, Walt Stanchfield, and John Ewing. One team of artists painted the colorful scenes against which the animated characters performed, and another created the layout designs.

Sterling Holloway, the well-known Hollywood character actor, spoke for Winnie the Pooh, while Sebastian Cabot handled the background narration. The director's ten-year-old son Bruce Reitherman was the voice of Christopher Robin. Richard M. and Robert B. Sherman, who won Oscars for their music for *Mary Poppins,* composed five songs for the *Pooh* film. The entire score was arranged and conducted by Buddy Baker.

All this for a twenty-six-minute cartoon—no wonder *Winnie the Pooh and the Honey Tree* has succeeded so well as a recreation in another medium of a treasured children's classic!

The

From Walt Disney's Motion Picture *The Jungle Book*,
inspired by the Rudyard Kipling "Mowgli" stories

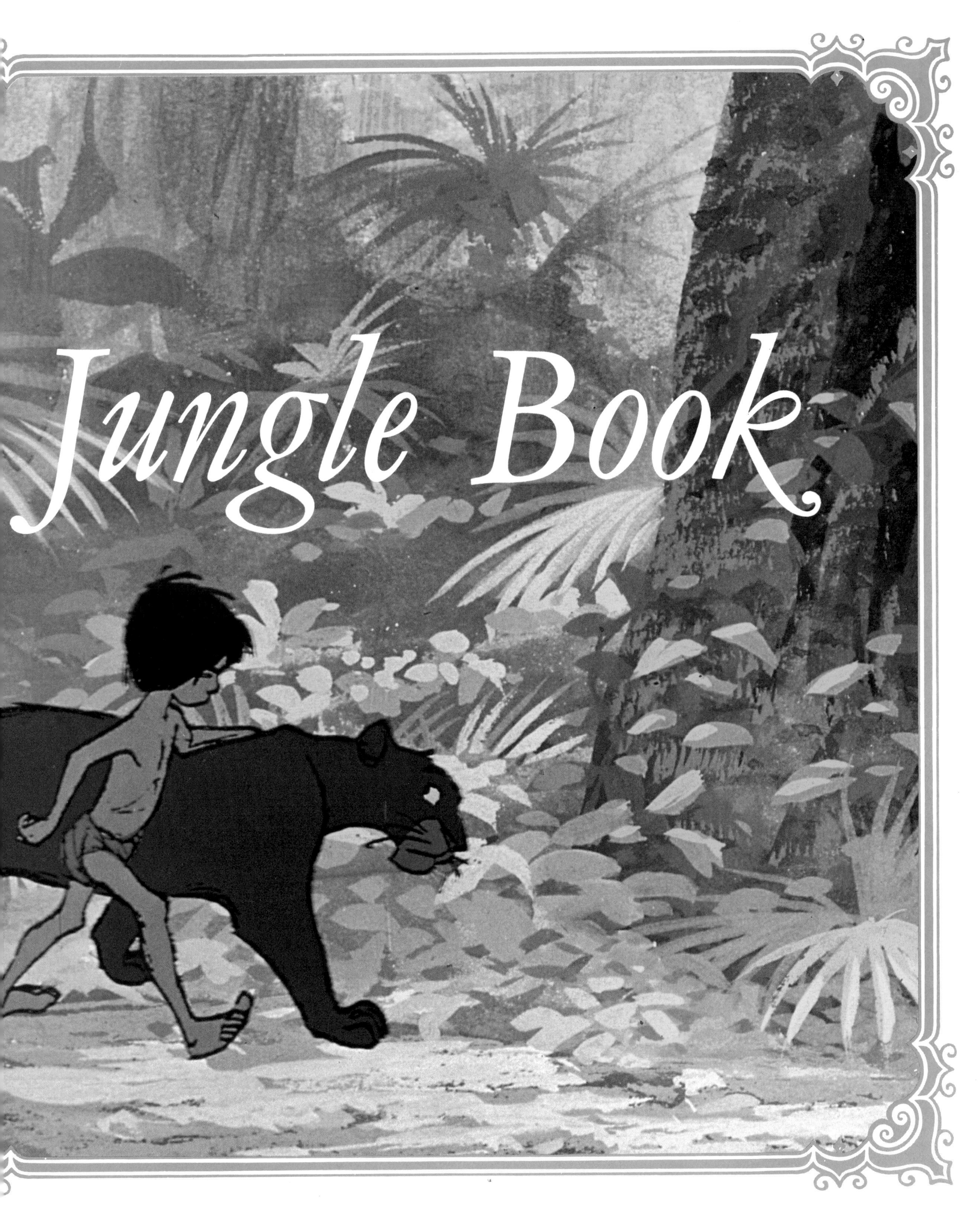
Jungle Book

any strange tales are told of the wild jungles in India, but none so strange as the story of Mowgli, the mancub, who was found by Bagheera, the black panther, in a basket by the riverbank. Bagheera carried the basket to a wolf family with young cubs and asked if they could feed and care for the mancub, too.

"I have never seen one," said Mother Wolf. "How little! How naked, and—how bold! See, he looks up and is not afraid."

The hungry little creature snuggled up to Mother Wolf with the other cubs. "Lie still, little frog," she told him. "Mowgli, Mowgli the Frog, I shall call you." And the wolves kept Mowgli and raised him like one of their own.

Ten times the rains had come, and Mowgli had grown as strong and hardy as his wolf brothers, with whom he had become a great favorite. Then, one night under a full moon, the elders of the Wolf Pack gathered at Council Rock for a very important meeting. Bagheera watched and listened from the limb of a nearby tree while they spoke. The Pack was alarmed because Shere Khan, a man-hating tiger, had returned to their jungle after a long absence. They feared he would surely kill the half-grown mancub and any wolves who tried to protect him.

Finally Akela, their leader, spoke. "It has been decided. The mancub can no longer stay with the Pack. It is too dangerous for the rest of us. He must leave at once." In vain Father Wolf pleaded that Mowgli could not possibly survive alone in the jungle. Then Bagheera, springing lightly from the tree, said he would take Mowgli to a man village several day's journey away, and leave him safely with his own kind.

Early the next morning Bagheera and Mowgli set out for a walk in the jungle. When night fell, Mowgli wanted to return to his wolf family, but the panther explained that he could not ever go back because Shere Khan had sworn to kill him. At this Mowgli grew very unhappy. "I *will* go back," he declared. "I can look after myself!" But the black panther would have no disobedience. "Enough," he growled. "We'll spend the night up in this tree. Things will look better in the morning."

No sooner had Bagheera dozed off than Kaa, a slippery python, slithered up the tree to the branch where Mowgli crouched, too unhappy to fall asleep. In the special way that pythons have, Kaa hypnotized Mowgli and coiled himself around his body. He was just about to open his jaws and swallow the mancub when Bagheera wakened. In a flash the panther knocked Kaa out of the tree and snatched Mowgli from him. "So, you can look after yourself, can you?" he sneered at the frightened mancub.

At daybreak Mowgli was awakened by a loud military voice shouting drill commands:

Hup, two, three, four,
Keep it up, two, three, four.
By the ranks or single file,
Over every jungle mile.

It was Colonel Hathi, the elephant, noisily drilling his troops. Mowgli, enjoying the new game, mischievously fell in behind the smallest baby elephant. But the Colonel saw him and trumpeted, "I say, what happened to your trunk?" Then, looking more closely, he bellowed, "A mancub! This is treason!" He knocked Mowgli to the ground and was about to stamp on him when Bagheera leapt between them. He apologized to the outraged elephant for Mowgli's bad manners and explained that he was taking him back to a man village.

But Mowgli still didn't want to go to the man village and he still missed his wolf family. He stubbornly grabbed a small tree and hung on while Bagheera tried to push and then to pull him on his way. In exasperation the black panther gave up. "All right, mancub," he snarled. "You're on your own," and he padded off into the jungle.

Mowgli sat down against a rock, alone and not quite sure which way to go next. While he was wondering, he heard a carefree song, and then the singer appeared. Baloo the bear came rollicking through the jungle, singing a jaunty song and dancing a few shuffling steps. He stopped short when he saw Mowgli. The bear and the mancub struck up a conversation, and sang and danced and played games together merrily. They went fishing, swam in the river, and had a fine lazy time. "Stay

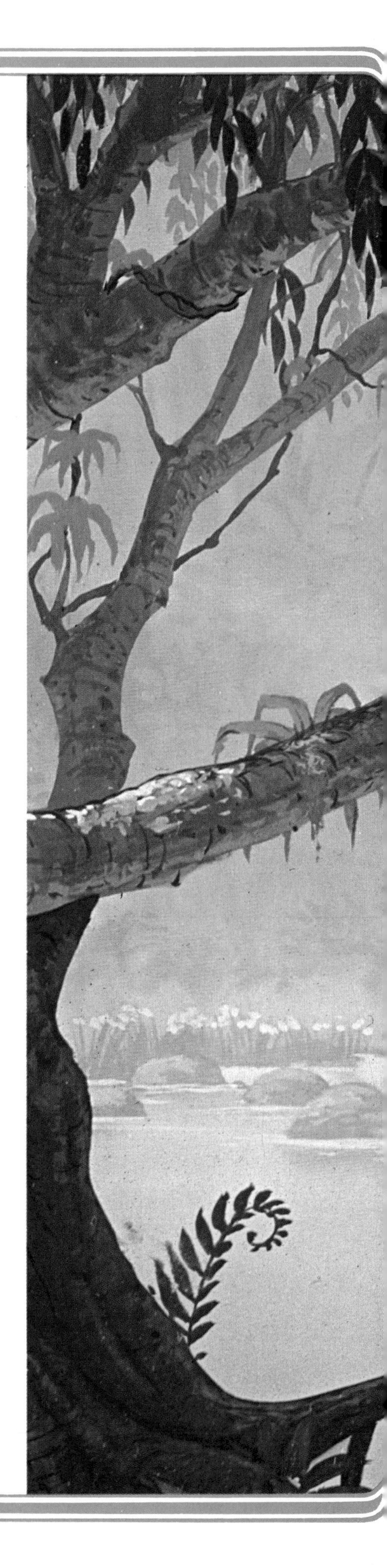

away from the man village," Baloo growled. "They'll ruin you. They'll make a man out of you. And you're going to make one swell bear."

All this time, a band of monkeys had been watching the two friends from high in the treetops. At a signal from their leader, two monkeys swiftly swung to the ground, grabbed Mowgli, and carried him off to the ruins of an ancient temple where their king, Louie, was waiting.

Meanwhile, Baloo called to Bagheera for help and, hoping to save the mancub, he and the panther raced through the jungle to the ruins. They were in time to hear King Louie demand that Mowgli give him the secret of Man's Red Flower. (By Red Flower the king meant fire, only no creature in the jungle will call fire by its proper name, since every beast lives in deadly fear of it.) But Mowgli didn't know how to grow the Red Flower and said so. Before the angry ape king could punish the mancub, his attention was caught by a large female ape dancing across the room. It was Baloo in disguise, waving and smiling at King Louie, and soon the infatuated ape king and all the monkeys were dancing wildly after

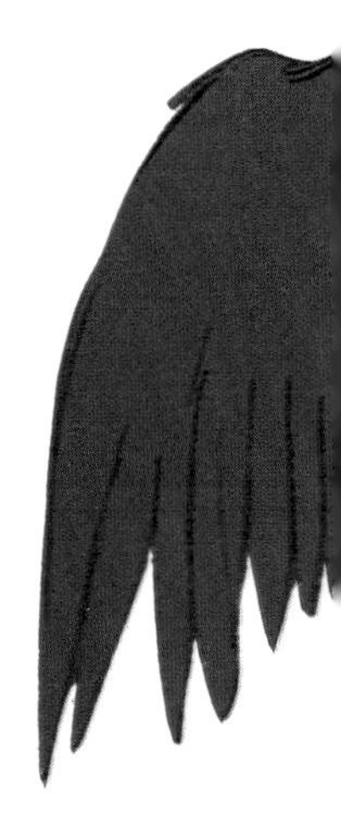

Baloo. The ruins shuddered and shook, and the temple pillars began to totter. Just before the building collapsed, Bagheera snatched Mowgli out of danger and in the confusion they and Baloo made their escape.

They were not to be together for long. Mowgli, fearing that Baloo also wanted him safely in the man village, ran away alone into the jungle. He wandered into a rocky place where a flock of ugly vultures had gathered. Seeing that the mancub was sad, the vultures tried to comfort him with jokes and funny dances. In the midst of their merrymaking, Shere Khan, the fierce tiger, stalked into the clearing. "Run, friend, run," the vultures shrieked as they flapped their wings and took off into the sky.

"I won't run from anyone," Mowgli declared. He picked up a club and prepared to hit the tiger. With a terrible roar, Shere Khan opened his mouth and bared his claws. Just as he was about to leap at the mancub, Baloo arrived, grabbed Shere Khan by the tail, and stopped him short, in mid-leap.

Meanwhile, the vultures returned to help Mowgli. One of them lifted the mancub in his powerful talons and flew off to a nearby tree, which had been struck by lightning and was aflame. "Fire, Mowgli, that's the only thing Old Stripes is afraid of. Get the Red Flower," he said, setting Mowgli on the ground. Mowgli picked up a burning branch and ran with it to Shere Khan. "Up, dog," he cried. "Up when a man speaks or I will set your coat ablaze."

Shere Khan snarled at the fire, and Mowgli beat him over the head with the branch, singeing his fur. The tiger, whimpering and whining in fear and pain, ran frantically across the clearing and disappeared over the farthest hill. "That is the last we'll see of him," said Baloo. "He took off like a flaming comet."

Toward evening, near the riverbank, Baloo and Mowgli were joined by Bagheera. The panther suggested that, with Shere Khan gone from the jungle, there was no reason why Mowgli couldn't remain with his animal friends forever. But Mowgli had felt a strange restlessness ever since he had held the stick abloom with the Red Flower. Something was different about him now. He knew he was meant to be a man and not a wolf.

And then a creature such as he had never seen before came down to the river, and as he watched her, Mowgli was captivated. Singing softly, she filled a vessel with water and placed it on her head. Mowgli approached her, took the vessel gently, and placed it on his own head, just as she had. The pretty creature walked along a little path that led to the man village, with Mowgli following. The sky was just beginning to darken when Mowgli entered the gates of the village to meet those mysterious things that are called men.

"Mowgli, come back, come back," called Baloo.

"Go on, go on," urged Bagheera.

Mowgli turned briefly, waved to his friends, and disappeared behind the village fence.

Baloo shrugged. "He would have made one swell bear," he said sadly.

THE JUNGLE BOOK

The Story of the Production

Inspired by Rudyard Kipling's Mowgli stories about a boy raised by wolves in the forests of India, *The Jungle Book,* released in 1967, was the last animated feature to be personally produced by Walt Disney. Thirty years and some seventeen animated movies after *Snow White,* the picture incorporated all of the advanced techniques and perfected artistic skills that the Studio had developed. Its lush and colorful jungle backgrounds are among Disney's most beautiful.

But the greatest innovation is how closely the animated characters are patterned after living personalities, whose voices are employed for the soundtrack. Phil Harris, with his easygoing traits, became Baloo, the happy-go-lucky bear; Louis Prima's gravel voice and jazz rhythms influenced the creation of King Louie, the jiving ape-potentate; George Sanders lent his suavely villainous personality to Shere Khan, the tiger; Sterling Holloway was the sneaky python, Kaa; Sebastian Cabot, the character actor, created the stern but dedicated panther, Bagheera; J. Pat O'Malley's Englishness was transmitted to Colonel Hathi, the elephant drilling his dawn patrol; and Bruce Reitherman, the youngster who was the voice of Christopher Robin in a Winnie the Pooh film, imprinted his endearing boyishness on young Mowgli. All of these actors, with their distinctive personalities, took command of the characters on the animators' drawing boards as in no other Disney picture.

The Jungle Book is an animated musical comedy that runs for an hour and eighteen minutes. The twelve sequences that make up the feature comprise 1,039 separate scenes and 760 painted backgrounds. And for every minute of animation there are 1,440 different pictures! These mind-boggling statistics are the reality behind Walt Disney's desire to make animation "a means of bringing life and motion to fine illustrations." They indicate why he was preeminently successful in creating fluid motion from drawings, rather than the flickering images that used to play across the movie screen in animated features.

Baloo the bear and his voice and model, Phil Harris, go into their song and dance

Contemporary Stories

Dumbo

From Walt Disney's Motion Picture *Dumbo,*
based on the book by Helen Aberson and Harold Pearl

The circus train was loaded and ready to start the trip north from winter quarters in Florida. But it was waiting for something. The clowns were ready, the acrobats were ready, nearly everyone was ready. The giraffes stuck their long necks through the roof of their car to find out the reason for the delay. Only the elephants knew why the train hadn't started, and the old gossips among them whispered the secret to one another. "It's Mrs. Jumbo. She's waiting for her baby."

Just then a stork carrying a large, heavy bundle flapped to a stop on the roof of the elephant car. "Well, little fella," he said to the bundle, "let's get going." Then he hollered, "Mrs. Jumbo! Calling Mrs.

Jumbo!" The other elephants waved their trunks through the hatch of the elephant car. "Over here, Stork," one of them trumpeted. The stork fluttered down to the floor of the car and deposited his bundle next to Mrs. Jumbo. "Here's your baby, Ma'am. Jumbo Jr."

Mrs. Jumbo carefully unwrapped the bundle. Smiling up at her was the most adorable blue-eyed baby elephant anyone had ever seen. The old gossips looked over the partition at the mother and her new baby. "Better than I expected," whispered one. "Isn't he adorable," said another. "Kootchy Kootchy," said a third, tickling the baby with her trunk.

At that, Jumbo Jr. sneezed—and when he sneezed his ears flopped forward. They were no ordinary large elephant ears; they were *enormous* ears, almost as big as the entire baby, and the gossips were horrified at first. Then they began to giggle and laugh at the funny-looking baby elephant. "Jumbo, indeed," giggled one. "He should be called DUMBO. That fits perfectly!"

But Mrs. Jumbo turned her back on them, wrapped the baby's ears around him, and cuddled Dumbo to her lovingly.

The circus train chugged along, and when it had to climb a mountain it struggled up the steep slope, panting, "I think I can, I think I can," and when it started down the other side it went faster and faster and huffed, "I thought I could, I thought I could." Finally the train stopped with a jolt at a little town. The circus people set up their tents and prepared to give their first show.

Dumbo watched the other elephants perform. They could do all kinds of wonderful tricks, balancing delicately with two feet on a ball or tub, standing on their hind legs with trunk raised in the air. Looking at them, Dumbo wondered if he could ever hope to perform such tricks.

His mother tried to protect him from the teasing of the circus folk and the people who came to see the "Biggest Little Show on Earth." But once they caught sight of the little elephant with the big ears people laughed. One day some children were especially unkind. When one boy actually started to pull Dumbo's ears it was too much for his mother. Mrs. Jumbo snatched the boy up and spanked him with her trunk. The Ringmaster ordered her chained, and when she tried to break loose to join Dumbo, the Ringmaster cried, "She's wild—tie down her trunk! Take her away! Put her in jail!"

Poor Dumbo. He was left alone in Mrs. Jumbo's empty stall. The other elephants would have nothing to do with him. "He's an F-R-E-A-K," they said, "and it's his fault Mrs. Jumbo is in jail." "Furthermore," said the leader of the gossips, "I wouldn't eat at the same bale of hay with him."

A tough little circus mouse named Timothy overheard all this unkind talk. "What's the matter with his ears?" he asked. "I think they're cute." Timothy decided Dumbo needed a friend and he would be it. But Dumbo trusted no one anymore, and he hid from Timothy in a haystack.

"Look, Dumbo, I'm your friend," said the mouse to the haystack. "Look what I've got for ya," and he held up a peanut. "C'mon out and be friends. Maybe together we could get your mother out of the clink."

Dumbo began to listen to Timothy, especially when the mouse explained that lots of people with big ears were famous. "Now look, Dumbo, if you're famous they don't make fun of ya. If they don't make fun of ya your ma don't get sore. If she don't get sore they let her outta jail—an' everything's OK!" Dumbo nodded. "So all we gotta do is make you a star! Dumbo the Great!" Timothy paused and scratched his whiskers. "The Great *What?*" he wondered.

Now it happened that the Ringmaster wanted to build the most sensational elephant act ever seen. Timothy overheard him talking about it. "In the ring stands seventeen elephants. One climbs up on top of another until all seventeen elephants makes a tremenjus Pyramid of Pachyderms. I blow the whistle, the trumpets are trumpeting, the drums are drumming—and then comes the climax." The trouble was, the Ringmaster had not yet figured out a tremendous climax. "Maybe it comes to me in a dream," he said.

That night Timothy whispered in the ear of the sleeping Ringmaster. "The climax for your Pyramid of Pachyderms is the Little Elephant with the Big Ears, the World's Mightiest Midget Mastodon, DUMBO! He will jump from a springboard to the very top of your pyramid, waving a flag for a glorious finish."

The next day the Ringmaster got his elephants together for the premiere of their dazzling act under the Big Top. Inspiration had come to him in a dream. Dumbo would be the climax. The pyramid of elephants was a bit wobbly but ready, Dumbo was dressed in a costume with a little flag to wave. The trumpets trumpeted, the drums rolled. "You're on, Dumbo," said Timothy, jabbing the reluctant elephant with a pin. Dumbo ran toward the springboard, but just as he got to it he tripped over his big floppy ears. Instead of sailing to the top of the high elephant pyramid he sailed smack into it, knocking the elephants off balance so they flew in all directions. One elephant landed on the high wire, two more found themselves bouncing up to the trapezes, one dropped into the safety net and its weight pulled the whole tent down. It was a disaster and Dumbo's clumsiness and big ears were to blame.

In disgrace Dumbo was sent to Clown Alley. "Oh, the shame of it," said one of the elephants. "Let us take the solemn vow," said another. "From now on Dumbo is no longer an elephant."

The clowns needed Dumbo to be the baby in their burning building act. Dumbo was terrified of the flames; he was afraid of jumping from the top-floor window to the firemen's net; and worst of all, he was ashamed to be a ridiculous plaything for the clowns.

But the audience loved the act with Dumbo in it. The clowns had never enjoyed such applause. After the show Timothy tried to cheer Dumbo. "You're a big hit. You're terrific. You're colossal." But Dumbo was still sad. "Look," said Timothy, "you were such a hit the clowns are drinking a toast to you." The clowns were celebrating their new success with champagne, and a bottle of it tipped over and spilled into Dumbo's water bucket.

Timothy and Dumbo innocently drank all the water, wondering at the strange bubbles in it. After an attack of hiccups, both fell asleep and Dumbo had a remarkable dream of pink elephants and flying. When Timothy and Dumbo awoke they were amazed to find themselves up on the limb of a tree, with a flock of Crows. They knew that elephants can't climb trees. There was only one way they could have arrived there—Dumbo must have *flown!*

Timothy became very excited. "Your ears, Dumbo. Dere poifect wings. You flew!"

But Dumbo didn't want to believe it. Finally, to help him, one of the Crows used some psychology. He gave Dumbo a Magic Feather to hold in his trunk. "Now you can fly," they all told him. Timothy sat in the rim of Dumbo's hat, and the Crows got behind the elephant on the branch of the tree and pushed. "Flap your ears," Timothy instructed. "Up, down—up, down—one, two, faster, faster. Get up your flying speed!" And Dumbo took off. "He fly just like a eagle!" exclaimed one Crow. "Better'n an airplane," said another. "Brother, now I've seen an elephant fly, I've seen everything!"

That day Dumbo made history. When he joined the clowns for the burning building act, instead of jumping from the top floor, Dumbo, with Timothy perched on his hat and the Magic Feather clutched in his trunk, FLEW. He flew all around the circus tent, looped up to the very top of it, zoomed down and around. The crowd, the clowns, the Ringmaster watched in amazement. Suddenly the Magic Feather blew away. Dumbo looked startled and stopped flapping his ears. "Come on

Dumbo, fly!" Timothy urged. "Open up them ears. The feather was just a gag. *You can fly,* honest, you can!"

Dumbo started to drop to the ground, but at Timothy's words he began to wave his big ears again—and he soared up, up, up, into the air. He could fly, he could really fly, all by himself!

"Wonder Elephant Soars To Fame," said the newspaper headline. "Dumbo Manager Signs Hollywood Contract." On the circus train Dumbo, Timothy, and Mrs. Jumbo, happy to be together at last, traveled in style in "Dumbo's Private Car." From that day on, Dumbo was the star of the circus.

DUMBO

The Story of the Production

Unlike Walt Disney's earlier animated features *Snow White, Pinocchio,* and *Fantasia, Dumbo* was in production only a little over a year. The picture was begun in 1940 and released in late 1941, a remarkable schedule for which there were several interesting reasons.

The original story, *Dumbo, the Flying Elephant,* by Helen Aberson and Harold Pearl, was simple, tightly constructed, and ideally suited to the animated screen, so the shooting script was developed quickly. Then the production team's enthusiasm for the picture carried them far beyond normal working hours, and their inspired overtime resulted in two or three times as much animation completed each week than for any previous feature.

The formidable technical problems that had had to be solved in each of the earlier features, using up a great deal of production time and dollars, had been mastered, and the resultant know-how was immediately available for *Dumbo.*

At this stage of the game, Walt Disney was familiar with his production artists' strengths, and he was able to cast them to their best advantage. The animators who created the unforgettable elephants in the "Dance of the Hours" sequence in *Fantasia* were turned loose on the elephants in *Dumbo.* But Disney did some less predictable casting, too. The artist responsible for Monstro the Whale in *Pinocchio* and the Devil in the "Night on Bald Mountain" sequence of *Fantasia* was chosen to animate the endearing, waiflike baby elephant, Dumbo, while the

A Disney artist, sketching at Cole Brothers' Circus, captures the authentic Big Top background

Working on the script of *Dumbo,* Joe Grant and Dick Huemer were inspired by a small model of the star

supervising artist of the lumbering dinosaurs in *Fantasia* was assigned to the tiniest, quickest, toughest member of *Dumbo*'s cast, Timothy Mouse.

The animators ran into an unusual problem in depicting elephants. They found that, when drawing close-ups, they had to deal with the big bulge of forehead, very small, wide-set eyes, and long proboscis, all of which made it difficult to convey emotions by means of subtle facial expressions. By taking liberties and bringing the features closer together, enlarging the eyes and fringing them with lashes, and emphasizing cheeks and jowls, which could move expressively, they solved the problem. Also, an elephant's mouth is usually hidden by its trunk, but the mouth must be seen if an animated elephant is talking. The artists got around that difficulty by having their elephants lift or gesture with their trunks while speaking. Thus the mouth could be seen, and the gestures gave added emphasis to the speech.

Dumbo never talked, but his expressions were eloquent, and his sidekick Timothy Mouse talked for both of them. Silent or not, Dumbo is one of the most successful and beloved of all the Disney characters.

Of the seven songs woven into the story line, "Casey Jr.," the train song, and "When I See an Elephant Fly" are outstanding favorites.

101

From Walt Disney's *101 Dalmatians,* based on *The Hundred and One Dalmatians* by Dodie Smith, published in the U.S. by The Viking Press, Inc., copyright 1956 by Dodie Smith, and in the United Kingdom by William Heinemann Limited

Dalmatians

ongo was a handsome white Dalmatian with black spots. He owned Roger Radcliff, a nice young bachelor musician who was gentle, obedient, and unusually intelligent. In fact, Pongo thought at times he was almost canine. Roger understood the barks for "Out, please!" "In, please!" "Where's my dinner?" and "Let's go for a walk." Pretty good for a human! They lived in a nice little house near Regents Park in London, but it had become very lonely for both of them.

To Pongo it was plain to see that his bachelor pet needed someone. He was too wrapped up in his work, writing songs all day and half into the night. Songs about romance, of all things, a subject he knew nothing about. So Pongo took matters into his own hands—or paws—and arranged a meeting in the park one spring day with Anita, a pretty lady who was owned by Perdita, a good-looking female Dalmatian. There's nothing like a walk in the park, in early spring, at dusk, when the lights are just blinking on all over London, to promote romance.

In a few short weeks there was a double wedding for Pongo and Perdita and Roger and Anita, and the dogs settled down to a life of pleasant domesticity with their happy pets.

The months passed peacefully, and in autumn Pongo and Perdita became the proud parents of their first litter of puppies. Fifteen beautiful little Dalmatians! When Roger saw the new puppies in the kitchen, where Nanny Cook was getting them settled, he was flabbergasted. "Fifteen puppies!" he exclaimed. "Why Pongo, boy, that's marvelous! You old rascal!" Pongo held his head high and there was a new light in his intelligent dark eyes.

Just then the doorbell rang and Nanny Cook opened it for Cruella De Vil, Anita's old schoolmate. No one liked her. She was mean and selfish, but Anita wanted to be polite to her. Cruella blew smoke in Anita's face and demanded, "Where are they?"

"Who, Cruella?" Anita asked. "The puppies, the puppies," Cruella said in a loud, rude voice. Anita picked up one of the tiny puppies. "I'll take them all, dear," said Cruella. "Just name your price." Cruella had a passion for fur coats, and she had her heart set on owning a white one with black spots. "I worship furs, I live for furs. Why, I even sleep between ermine sheets. That's why I *must* have these Dalmatians."

But Roger, who had just come into the room, said firmly, "We aren't selling the puppies and that's final!" Pongo stood by, nodding his head. "Not even one," Roger added. "No, no, and NO again."

"You'll be sorry," Cruella shouted. "I'll get even with all of you.

Fools! Idiots!" And she slammed the door behind her with a crash that broke the glass.

Anita embraced Roger. "Oh, darling, you were magnificent," she said. Roger puffed on his pipe. "That's a strange name, De Vil. If you put both parts together it spells Devil. Maybe that's why she's so mean." Pongo ran to the pantry to tell Perdita the good news. "My ole pet Roger. He told her off, Perdy. She's gone for good!"

One evening about six weeks later, Pongo and Perdita took Roger and Anita for their customary evening walk in the park. The puppies were at home, watching television before bedtime, when the back doorbell rang most unexpectedly. When Nanny Cook answered it, there stood a tall skinny man with a poker and a short fat man with a club. "Uh, we're from the gas company," said the short one; his tall partner pushed past him into the kitchen. While Nanny Cook protested, the two thugs locked her in the cellar, scooped up fifteen sleepy puppies, and stuffed

them into a large burlap bag. They carried the bag to a van waiting outside, and off they sped.

Half an hour later Pongo and Perdita brought Roger and Anita back and heard Nanny Cook banging on the cellar door. After they freed her they all searched the house to see what silver or valuables had been stolen. Everything was in its proper place except the puppies. Of the fifteen spotted Dalmatians there wasn't a trace. "Those scoundrels! They stole the puppies!" wailed Nanny Cook.

Roger was very good. He was on the phone to the police, to Scotland Yard, to the newspapers to place ads and offer "reward for return, no questions asked." The next day Cruella De Vil telephoned. "Oh, Anita," she crooned, "what a dreadful thing. I just saw the papers. Have the police been any help?" But before Anita could answer politely, Roger grabbed the phone. "Where are they, Cruella?" he demanded. "Idiot!" Cruella screamed. But Pongo, standing near the phone, nodded his head in agreement with Roger. He, too, thought Cruella was the number one suspect, although there was no proof so far.

That evening, while Perdita slept next to him, exhausted by grief, Pongo chewed on the wicker of his basket as Roger might thoughtfully smoke his pipe. In spite of his playful, charming ways, Pongo happened to possess one of the keenest brains in dogdom, and he used it now. He devised a plan.

The next day the police and Scotland Yard had nothing to report. Pongo took Perdita into his confidence. "Perdy," he said, "I'm afraid it's all up to us dogs. We must use the Twilight Bark." That is the dogs' way of keeping in touch with other canines, however distant, of passing on important news or just plain gossip.

It was a few weeks before Christmas and twilight came early. Pongo and Perdita made their wish clear to take Anita and Roger for a walk just before dusk. With the Radcliffs firmly attached to their leashes, the two Dalmatians eagerly led the way to Regents Park. At the top of a little hill Pongo and Perdita stood side by side. They barked to the south, north, east, and west, and from the distance answering barks could be heard. "Perdy, we're in luck. It's the Great Dane at Hampstead. He has a network of friends throughout the country," Pongo reported after one especially clear bark. The All Dog Alert was on its way, with news of the stolen puppies being relayed all across England. Every dog who heard it would turn detective, and their answers could be expected the following evening.

From the Great Dane to a terrier, to a Scottie, to an Afghan puppy, to a barge dog of no discernible bloodlines but much intelligence, to a goose on the river, to a horse in a barn in Suffolk, to the barnyard cat

named Tibs, to a shaggy old dog with the habit of command, called "Colonel"—the chain of dogs relayed the message. *"Fifteen spotted puppies dognapped from London!"*

"Colonel, Sir," said Tibs the cat, "two nights past when I was prowling about, I thought I heard puppies barking over at Hell Hall, the old abandoned De Vil place." "By Jove!" exclaimed the Colonel. "There is smoke coming from the chimney, and where there's smoke there's fire. We'd better see what's up."

Under cover of darkness the Colonel and Tibs stole up to the old house. Tibs crawled through an open window and found himself in a room full of little Dalmatians. "Are you the fifteen stolen puppies?" he asked. "No, we're bought and paid for," one of the puppies answered. "All eighty-four of us. There's another bunch of little ones in the other room. They're watching T.V. with the Badun Brothers."

"Watch out for the Baduns!" warned one of the pups. "They're mean."

Tibs slipped quietly into the next room. There he saw a tall thin man and a short fat one, both with disagreeable faces. Tibs was able to count fifteen black-and-white-spotted puppies scattered about the room. The kidnapped Dalmatians! He flashed the good news to the Colonel through the open window. Back through the chain of dogs it traveled to the Great Dane in Hampstead.

The next evening in Regents Park, Pongo and Perdita heard the message, and late that night they started their journey to Suffolk to rescue their children. It took them two nights of steady running, mile after snowy mile, since they dared not show themselves in daylight. Dogs along the way, who had been alerted by the Twilight Bark, gave them food, shelter, directions, and news of the puppies. At last on a cold frosty night Pongo and Perdita found the Colonel, up to his neck in a snowdrift, keeping watch at the gates of Hell Hall.

They were just in time! The Baduns had received orders from Cruella to kill all ninety-nine Dalmatians that very night, and the brothers were trying to capture the frightened puppies. They had chased them from room to room in the dark old house, but that clever cat Tibs had led the puppies to safety every time while leading the Baduns a merry chase. Now at last, the brothers had the whole kit and caboodle cornered in the Red Room. Escape was no longer possible.

But at the very instant that one of the Baduns was saying, "Now we got 'em!" two snarling furies crashed through the window and hurled themselves at the men. Perdita fastened her jaws on the club that was raised against her darlings; Pongo went after one of the Baduns, who yelled, "I'll knock the spots off of ya, ya mongrel." The ninety-nine puppies set up a racket, but Tibs led them out through the open window in a safe and orderly retreat to the old barn.

The puppies and their parents had a happy reunion there while the Colonel stood guard outside, prepared to hold the Baduns at bay. "Are all fifteen of you here?" asked Pongo. "Twice as many," said one of his puppies. "There are ninety-nine of us now." And they told how Cruella had bought up all the Dalmatians she could find because she wanted to make coats of them. "They were going to pop us off and skin us!" said one of the pups. "Dogskin coats is what she was after."

Perdita and Pongo were shocked, and they talked together softly. Then Pongo announced, "We'll take you all home with us. Our pets would never turn you out." The Colonel called out, "Better be off. Here they come!"

So Pongo, Perdita, and all the little Dalmatians, after thanking their new friends, set off across the snow-covered fields for the long trip home.

Unfortunately one hundred and one dogs leave a lot of tracks in the snow—four hundred and four paw prints, to be exact. And Cruella (who had driven up from London expecting to collect her dogskins) and the Baduns in their van would have very little trouble following Pongo and Perdita and their charges. Halfway to London, a jet black Labrador ran out of his village with good news for Pongo. There was a truck leaving for London with room for all of them. "A ride home, everyone!" barked Pongo. "Did you hear that?"

Immediately the cold and tired puppies were cheered. The Labrador led them to a warm blacksmith's shop to wait until the truck was ready to leave. Just then they heard the roar of a motor and Cruella De Vil's red car drove slowly past, trailed by the Baduns' van. They were following the dogs' tracks and stopped near the blacksmith's shop. "Idiots!" Cruella screamed. "They've got to be near here somewhere. Find them!"

"Oh, Pongo," said Perdita, "what shall we do?" But one of their puppies accidentally found the answer. He fell into the blacksmith's ashes and in an instant became completely black. "Look," said Pongo, "he's a Labrador! Let's all do the same. Cruella is looking for Dalmatians." So all the dogs rolled in the ashes, and then one hundred and one sooty black Labradors marched out to the truck, right past Cruella's car and the Baduns' van. "I've always wanted to get good and dirty," giggled one of the pups. But just as the last of the pups was being helped into the truck by Pongo, some melting snow from the roof dropped onto it, washing off the soot and showing the white fur with black spots.

"There they go!" screamed Cruella. "My dogs! My coats! After the little mongrels," she yelled to the Baduns.

But the truck had started on its way to London, with all the dogs safely inside. Cruella's red car sped after it, with snow flying from its wheels. The Baduns were right behind her. Cruella tried to ram into the truck, but the driver yelled "Crazy woman driver!" and raced his truck across a narrow bridge well ahead of her. Cruella's car skidded wildly, the Baduns' van crashed into it, and both flipped over into a ditch. The last the cheering Dalmatians heard of Cruella was her furious voice floating up from the ditch, addressing the Baduns, "You idiots! You fools! You imbeciles!"

When the truck reached London the Dalmatians headed straight for the house near Regents Park. Nanny Cook opened the door to see what all the barking was about, and she was nearly knocked over by a wave of happy black dogs. Roger said, "Why, they're Labradors." But Anita recognized Perdita, then Pongo, then some of the pups. They cleaned them up as best they could and counted them as best they could.

"One hundred and one!" Roger exclaimed. "Pongo, you old rascal!" "We'll have to buy a bigger place in the country," said Anita. "We'll have a plantation," Roger hummed. Then he sat down at the piano and sang:

We'll have a plantation,
A Dalmatian plantation,
Where our population can roam.

And they all joined in singing Roger's newest, jolliest song.

101 DALMATIANS

The Story of the Production

Animals and comedy, two of the Disney Studio's strong points, are combined in this sophisticated thriller about a dognapping case solved by dogs. Based on a successful British novel by Dodie Smith, the picture was released in 1961 after nearly three years in production, at a total cost of $4 million.

It is possible that the 150 studio artists labored so long because of the unique nature of the characters. Dalmatians wear white coats with black spots, and, according to Studio statistics, the creation of 101 of them entailed the laborious painting of a total of 6,469,952 spots! For those interested in the minutiae of animation technique, Pongo, the leading canine character, wears 72 black spots while Perdita, his mate, sports a coat with but 68; each of the 99 puppies wears 32.

This film was the first to use a reproduction process known as Xerography, in which the artists' drawings were transferred directly to

Frank Thomas, animal animator extraordinary, makes sketches for *101 Dalmatians* with the assistance of five of them

The spontaneity of the delightful sketches made from live models has been preserved by the Xerox camera, which transfers the animators' drawings directly to the cels

the cels (transparent overlays on which the characters are drawn), and from them to the film. The laborious hand-inking of thousands of cels was, therefore, no longer necessary.

One of the most impressive comic effects was the smoke emanating in curls and clouds from villainess Cruella De Vil's ever-present cigarette. Waved about in a slinky long holder, the cigarette created its own calligraphy of evil. The special effects technicians used so much smoke that, if it were compressed into a single cloud, they estimate it would blanket a city of one hundred thousand souls.

Rod Taylor, a rugged Australian actor, supplied the voice for Pongo, the picture's hero; the slightly higher tones of Ben Wright served for Roger Radcliff, the human second lead. J. Pat O'Malley was responsible for four of the "character" voices and a good deal of the authentic Cockney slang.

Not surprisingly, in a picture dealing in part with a songwriter, the songs are clever and catchy. "Playful Melody," "Cruella De Vil," and "Dalmatian Plantation" are among the brightest.

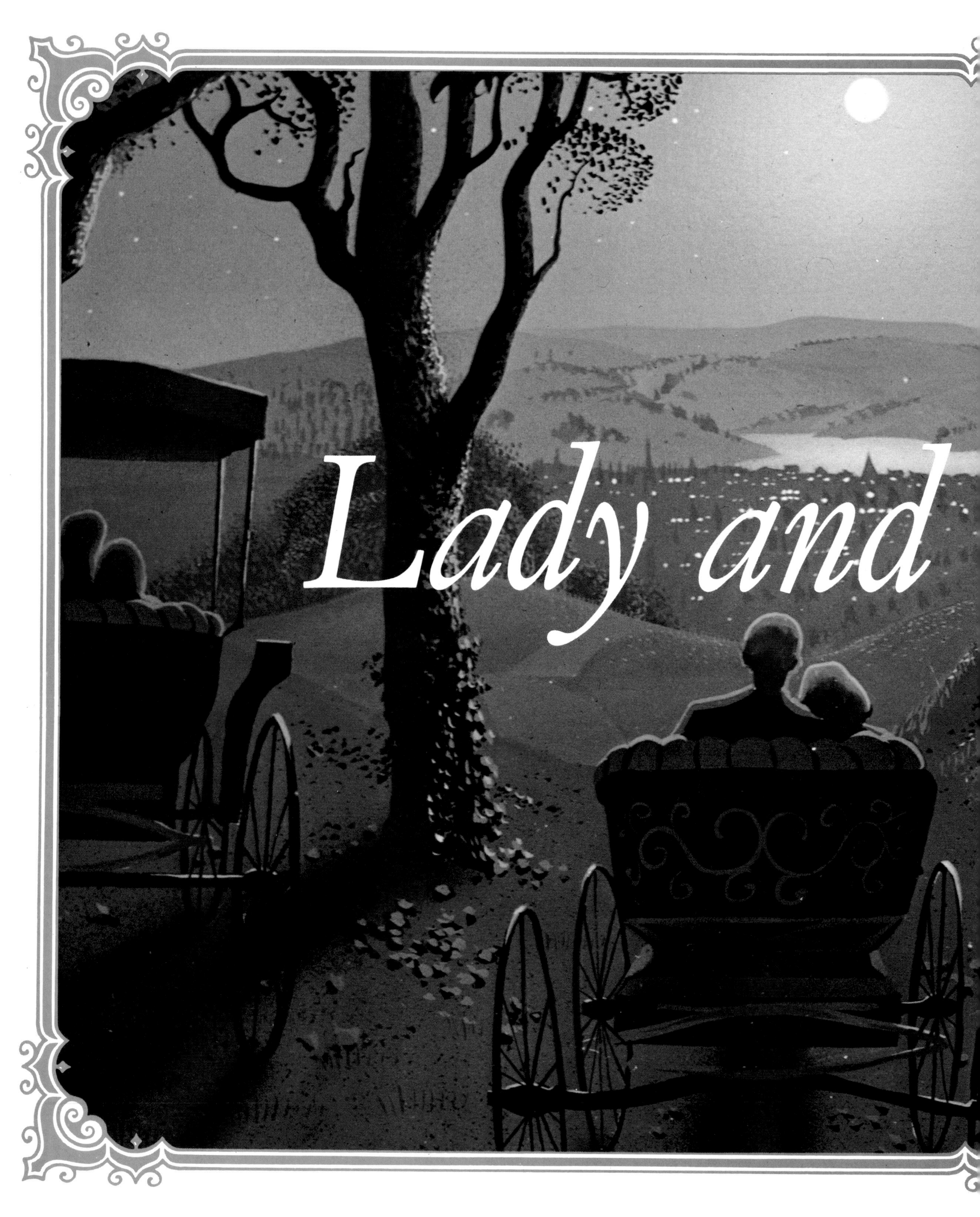

Lady and

the Tramp

From Walt Disney's Motion Picture *Lady and the Tramp*,
from the story by Ward Greene

t was Christmas day of the year 1910 in a small American town, a very special Christmas for a young couple because it was their first one together. Jim Dear handed his wife Darling a gift box tied with a big ribbon. When Darling opened it a little cocker spaniel puppy peeked out. "Oh, I love her!" Darling exclaimed. "What a perfectly beautiful little lady!" And that is how Lady got her name.

On Christmas night Jim Dear and Darling tucked Lady into her own little basket with her own little cover. Then they turned out the lights and went upstairs to bed. Lady climbed out of the basket and followed them, howling. Three times they brought her back downstairs. Finally, being intelligent people, they understood. From that night on, Lady slept on their bed.

It was a happy life. Each morning, after waking Jim Dear, Lady would dash out through her own little door and bring in the mail and the newspaper. All day, while Jim Dear was away, she policed the yard and kept the house safe by chasing away blackbirds, butterflies, and anything or anyone she thought dangerous. In the evening when she heard Jim Dear's whistle she raced to meet him, then she raced him to the front door. Jim Dear, who was always polite, would say, "Ladies first," as he opened the front door for her. At night, when the three of them sat around the fireplace together, Lady thought there could be no happier family in all the world.

Her two best friends were Jock, an elderly Scottie who lived next door, and Trusty, an aging Southern bloodhound who lived across the street. One day they were joined by a stranger in town, a carefree, cocky mongrel named Tramp. Her friends noticed that something was troubling Lady and tried to help her. Jim Dear and Darling were expecting a baby and, said Lady sadly, they seemed to have lost all interest in her. "Weel now, Lassie, I wouldna worry muh wee head about that," Jock tried to comfort her.

"You see, Miss Lady," Trusty explained. "There comes a time in the life of all humans when, well, like with the birds and the bees, a stork comes, and brings a cute little bundle of joy. But they'll still love you, too. Why, Miss Lady, everybody knows a dog's best friend is his human."

Lady was cheered a little but then the stranger, Tramp, spoke up and what he said was exactly what was worrying Lady. "Remember this, Pigeon," Tramp pointed out, "when a baby moves in, the dog moves out." Poor Lady! Tears sprang to her lovely brown eyes. Tramp continued, "That nice warm bed by the fire? Forget it, you'll wind up in a leaky doghouse."

Jock was furious with the stranger for upsetting his friend. "Off with ye," he barked. "We've no need of mongrels here and their r-r-radical ideas!"

Lady thought about Tramp's warning a lot during the next months. Then one April night there was great excitement in the little house. The doctor came and stayed quite a while. Jim Dear ran up and down the stairs and hardly noticed Lady. After a time a strange sound came from Darling's room, a kind of whimpering cry. Jim Dear ran out yelling happily, "It's a boy! It's a boy!"

For a few days Lady was kept out of the bedroom she used to share with Jim Dear and Darling because the baby lived there with them. She could hear Darling singing soft sweet songs, and Jim Dear would lower his voice and walk on tiptoe when he entered the room. Lady stood guard out in the hall, but one evening Jim Dear patted her head and said, "It's high time you met the rest of the family, Lady," and he brought her over to the cradle. Darling, looking happier and more beautiful than ever, was singing the baby to sleep. As she and Jim Dear and Lady looked down at the little pink creature, they were a happy family once more. Lady wagged her tail joyfully. Tramp had been all wrong.

About a month later Jim Dear and Darling were packing their suitcases for a short trip. Jim's Aunt Sarah was coming to look after the baby. "Don't worry, old girl," Jim said to Lady. "We'll be back in a few days and you'll be here to help Aunt Sarah."

But the first thing Aunt Sarah did after she arrived was to chase Lady out of the room. "Shoo! Shoo! Scat! Get out of here! You'll frighten the baby." No one had ever spoken to Lady like that before. Her feelings were hurt, and sadly she went downstairs to be by herself for a while.

In the living room an astonishing sight greeted Lady. There was Aunt Sarah's basket, and out of it slithered two of the slinkiest creatures Lady had ever seen. Slyly they looked at her and purred:

We are Siamese, if you please,
We are Siamese, if you don't please.
We are looking over our new domicile.
If we like, we stay for maybe quite a while.

Then the two cats leapt about the room and did the most outrageous things, mischief that the well-brought-up Lady would never have dreamed of. They climbed the birdcage stand, they jumped on the sofa cushions, they slid on the piano, scratching its polished surface with their sharp claws, they frightened the wits out of the goldfish when they tried to catch it. Then they started up the stairs to find the baby's milk.

Lady, horrified, could stand no more. She barked furiously and went after the cats. Guests or no guests, they could not be allowed to wreck her family's house and steal the baby's milk. Aunt Sarah heard the commotion and stormed down the stairs. There were her precious cats, chased to the top of the bookshelf by that vicious dog who had made the room an absolute shambles.

"Oh, you wicked animal!" Aunt Sarah scolded. "Attacking my poor innocent little angels!" And she hauled Lady off to a pet store and had her muzzled and leashed.

Terrified of the strange leather straps enclosing her face, Lady broke away and ran out of the pet store. She was in a strange neighborhood and had run only about a block when a pack of vicious dogs caught sight of her and gave chase. They pursued her into an alley and had her cornered when Tramp, who was lunching nearby and recognized Lady, leapt between her and the charging dogs. He was an old street brawler from

way back and, fighting furiously, he beat off the pack of dogs and chased them away.

"What are you doing in this rough part of town, Pigeon?" he asked Lady. Then he saw the muzzle. "We've gotta get that thing off. I know just the place." Taking Lady's leash in his mouth he led her to the zoo. Lady was so grateful to be protected by a big strong dog that she asked no questions.

When they reached the zoo, they went first to the alligator's cage. One look at his mouthful of teeth, and they decided to try something smaller. At the beaver's pond Tramp announced, "There's the answer to our problem." Sure enough, the beaver, though busy, was happy to oblige. With his strong front teeth, which could chew through trees, he made quick work of chewing through the leather straps—and the muzzle fell off. "Ya can keep it, friend, it's all yours," said Tramp, while Lady laughed for the first time in ages.

To celebrate, Tramp took Lady to dinner at Tony's Italian restaurant. Tony and his chef serenaded the romantic couple, and Tramp asked Lady if she would stay with him and share his happy-go-lucky life. "We'd be footloose and collar-free," he said. "It sounds wonderful," Lady sighed, "but who'd watch over the baby?" She had made a promise to Jim Dear and Darling, and she could not break it. So Tramp sadly agreed to take her home.

At home, Lady was in disgrace and Aunt Sarah forced her to stay in the doghouse, away from the baby and her precious cats. It was a rainy

night, and the doghouse leaked. Miserably, Lady kept watch over her snug warm home where a light burned in the baby's window. Suddenly she saw a dark shape scurry across the yard and up the trellis to the baby's room. A rat! Frantically she barked a warning, but Aunt Sarah only called out, "Lady, stop that racket this minute, or you'll be sorry!"

But Tramp heard the noise several blocks away and came running to see if Lady was in trouble. "A rat in the baby's room!" she told him. They both rushed to the house, squeezed in through Lady's little door, and quickly climbed the stairs to the baby's room. Tramp chased the rat all around the room, and the baby's crib was overturned, but the infant was unharmed. While Lady watched over the baby, Tramp cornered the rat at last behind the curtains and killed it.

Lady was so proud of him, and so relieved that the baby was safe. But Aunt Sarah, disturbed by the noise, came into the room, saw the overturned crib and the strange mongrel, and screamed, "Merciful Heavens! You vicious brutes!" She locked Lady in a closet and chased Tramp to the cellar. "That's it," Aunt Sarah declared. "Now I'm going to call the dogcatcher."

Tramp was taken away in the dogcatcher's wagon, and was to be destroyed the next day. Luckily, Jim Dear and Darling returned home not long after. When they released Lady from the closet she barked so urgently that Jim asked, "What is it, old girl? What are you trying to tell us?" Lady rushed over to the curtains and barked louder. Jim lifted a corner of the curtain and there lay the dead rat. Then they understood everything.

Jim immediately set out after the dog wagon but Jock and Trusty were ahead of him. Their barking made the horses bolt, and the wagon overturned. Jim Dear, arriving on the scene, said to the dogcatcher, "There's been a mistake. That dog is mine!" And he freed Tramp and brought him home to a hero's welcome.

And now it is another Christmas and the baby has grown, but so has the family. Jim Dear and Darling have quite a time getting them all in a Christmas picture, all holding still at the same time. There's Baby, and Lady, and Tramp—proudly wearing a collar, too—and four little pups. Three of them look just like their gentle mother, but the fourth one, Scamp, is a chip off the old block.

LADY AND THE TRAMP

The Story of the Production

Walt Disney wanted to do a dog story about a pretty little cocker spaniel named Lady and her human family as seen through her eyes. "We discovered during our preliminary conferences that we had only half the story we wanted," said Walt. "Our prim, well-bred and house-sheltered little Lady, when confronted with a crisis, just up and ran away, and all our cajoleries couldn't lure her back again. We had forgotten one all-important thing—a dog is entitled to some natural animal life aside from being man's best friend and his most tolerant critic. It was when we ignored this that we got into trouble storywise and dogwise."

Then Disney read a story by Ward Greene about a raffish dog, "Happy Dan, the Whistling Dog," and it struck him that a dog like Greene's mutt, who wore no man's collar, might be the perfect foil for Lady. He got in touch with the author, they conferred, "and exchanged doggish anecdotes and family experiences involving our own pets. It wasn't long before Ward had whistled up the Tramp and," said Disney, "it didn't take much urging to incite Ward to write a book about their amazing adventures, upon which we based our picture."

Peggy Lee, the singer and composer, wrote five of the picture's songs with Sonny Burke. She sang "He's a Tramp," the lullaby "La-La-Lu," and the unforgettable "Siamese Cat Song."

One of Walt Disney's innovations in the making of this feature was to construct a miniature Victorian Gothic mansion, furnished down to the last detail. Celluloid cutouts of the principal characters, in the proper scale, were used to work out positioning and relationship to the backgrounds. Everything was to be shown through the eyes of the canine characters, from a very low angle, and the model house helped solve problems of perspective. It also unified the work of the picture's many artists and directors—all backgrounds and furniture were identical on every drawing board. Most important, the scale model was used in choosing interesting angles and composing the shots for the CinemaScope process.

Released in 1955, this is the first Disney cartoon feature to use the broad expanse of CinemaScope. Partly as a result of the new technical problems introduced by the wide screen, the picture required four years and cost $4 million to make.

Surrounded by storyboard sketches of the Siamese cat sequence, Peggy Lee sings the "Siamese Cat Song," delighting a trio of the film's artists and directors

From Walt Disney Productions' Motion Picture *The Aristocats,*
based on a story by Tom McGowan and Tom Rowe

The Aristocats

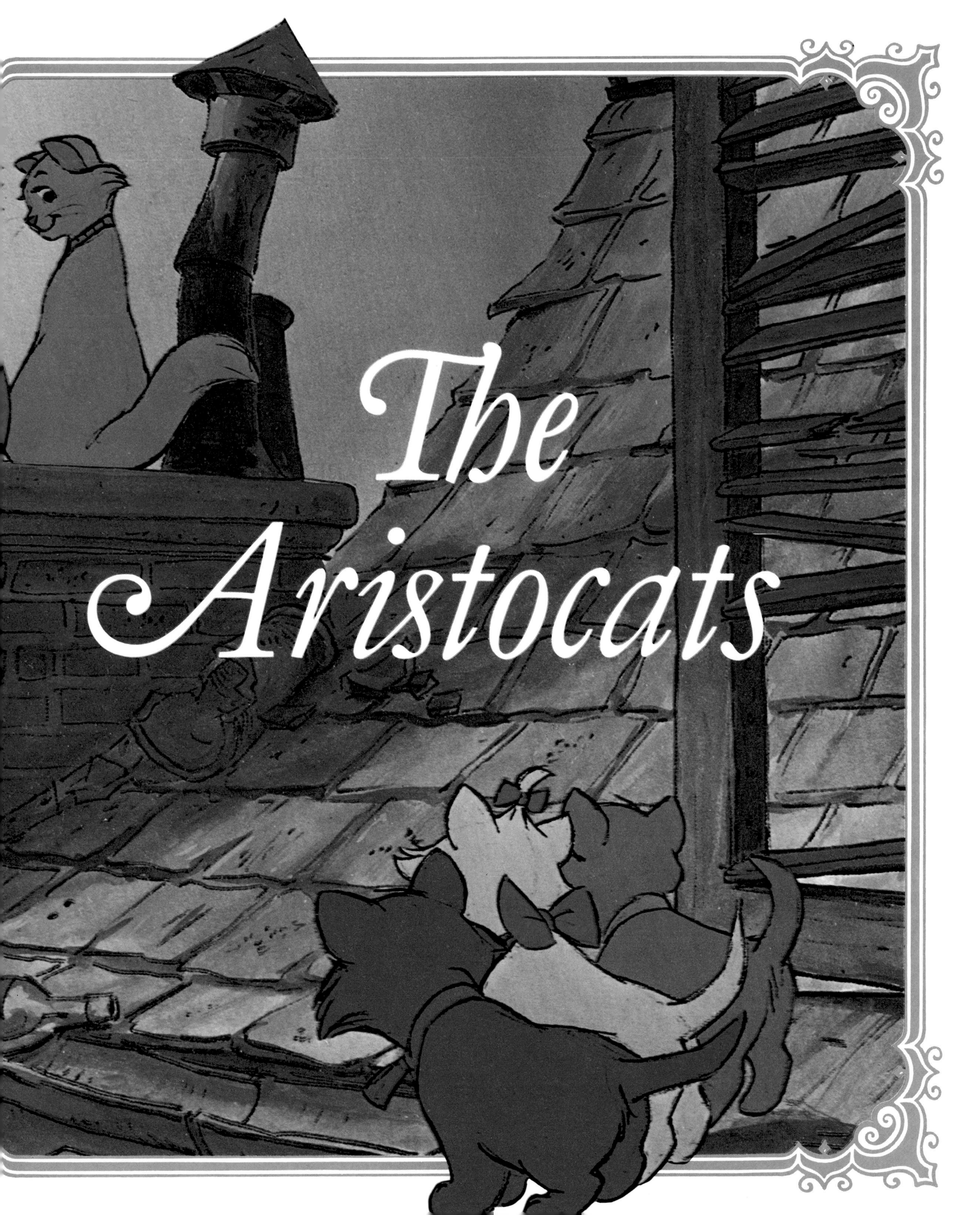

In the beautiful city of Paris, quite a long time ago, lived a wealthy old lady and her family of cats. There was Duchess, the mother cat, and her three mischievous kittens, Berlioz, Toulouse, and Marie. On fine spring days Madame Bonfamille would ask her butler, Edgar, to bring around the open carriage so that she and the cats could go for a drive.

At home, on a tree-lined street of elegant mansions, there were wonderful things for Duchess and her kittens to play with: a grand piano, a new-fangled phonograph, balls of fluffy yarn. They were served the very best food on silver trays, and they slept in their own canopied bed in Madame's room. These were no ordinary cats, you may be sure—they were *aristocats.*

Madame loved her cats and she wanted to be certain they would enjoy the good life even after she was gone. So one day she called her lawyer, the oldest in Paris, and asked him to drive right over to help her make her will.

"I want to leave my entire fortune to my cats," she explained after she had greeted the lawyer. "While they live, my faithful servant Edgar will take good care of them."

"Leave everything to your cats, Madame?" asked the lawyer, astonished.

"Yes," Madame Bonfamille said firmly, "that's what I wish. Then, at the end of their lives, everything can go to Edgar."

The butler had been listening to this conversation through the speaking tube in his room. At first he was pleased, but then he thought, "Cats first, and I come after the cats. That's not fair!"

The more Edgar thought about Madame's fortune the greedier he became. He did not want to wait to inherit it from Duchess and the kittens. "Those cats have got to go," he decided, "so I can get the fortune first."

That evening Edgar put a drug in the cats' milk. He waited until it had done its work and the cats were in a deep sleep. Then he sneaked them out of the house in a basket, climbed onto his motorcycle, and sped off to the country, where he planned to drown the cats in the first river he came to.

But two farm dogs spoiled his plans. Aroused by the motorcycle's racket, the dogs chased Edgar, barking and snarling right behind him. In his fright, Edgar dropped the basket of sleeping cats, and he didn't dare turn back for it or stop until he was safely home in Paris.

It was still dark when Duchess and her kittens awoke to find themselves in a very strange place—the country. "Why, we're not home at all," Duchess said. The kittens were frightened by the unfamiliar country

noises, and they thought they had had a bad dream. "We were all riding," said Toulouse. "And bouncing along," Berlioz added. "Yes," said Marie, "and Edgar was in the dream."

Toulouse had a thought. "It wasn't a dream! Edgar really did this to us."

"Oh," Berlioz mewed. "I wish we were home with Madame right now."

"Poor Madame," Duchess sighed, "she'll be so worried when she finds us gone."

When daylight came, Duchess saw that they were under a bridge near a river. And on the opposite bank of the river a large ginger cat was strutting along doing some nifty steps and singing a jolly song. "I'm O'Malley, the alley cat," he caterwauled:

I've got that wanderlust,
Gotta kick up highway dust,
Gotta strut them city streets,
Showin' off my éclat.
I'm O'Malley, the alley cat.

Duchess thought he was quite the handsomest cat she had ever seen. When he finished his song and sat down on a rock near her she applauded. "You are a great talent," she told him. "I liked your song."

"Thanks, Baby," said O'Malley. "I got a million of 'em." He was about to sing her another, but Duchess was worried about finding her way back to Paris with the kittens, and she told him of her troubles.

O'Malley gallantly offered to lead them all back to Paris. "And when we get there," he promised, with a twinkle, "I'll show you the time of your life." The kittens were thrilled, but Duchess explained that her mistress would be worried about them, and they had to return to her as quickly as possible. "You see, she loves us very much. Poor Madame, in that big mansion all alone." And she wiped a tear from her eye with the end of her fluffy white tail.

O'Malley led them to the railroad tracks, which stretched in two long silver lines all the way to Paris. The kittens hopped up on one of the rails. "Let's play train! I'm the engine!" said Berlioz, jumping ahead of Toulouse and Marie. "And Marie has to be the caboose."

With a loud "choo, choo, choo, choo" and a "clickety, clickety, clack, whoo, whoo," the entire family of cats progressed in single file toward Paris, Duchess and O'Malley following the kittens. They were crossing a trestle bridge high above the river when they heard the whistle of a *real* train and the clickety-clack of *real* wheels speeding toward them. "All right now, don't panic," O'Malley ordered, and he showed them how to scramble off the tracks and hang on for dear life underneath the trestle while the train thundered by overhead. It was a narrow escape!

They reached the outskirts of Paris that evening and walked along the rooftops of some old houses. The kittens and Duchess, who were used to being driven in a carriage for even the shortest distances, were weary and footsore. "I'm tired, mama," whined Marie. "Me, too, and my feet hurt," Berlioz complained. "I'll bet we've walked a thousand miles!" said Toulouse.

"Keep your whiskers up, Tiger," O'Malley said cheerfully. "My pad is just beyond that next chimney, and you can stay there tonight." He carried little Marie on his back. "It's not exactly the Ritz," he explained as they approached his window, "but it's peaceful and quiet—" The rest of O'Malley's sentence was drowned out by the sounds of some of the loudest, hottest jazz in all Paris.

"Oh, no!" said O'Malley. "My friend Scat Cat and his gang have dropped by and they're real swingers." Duchess and her kittens forgot how tired they were when they heard the music, and they eagerly climbed through the window to meet the band. Before long all had joined in the bouncy rhythms and were singing with Scat:

Everybody wants to be a cat
Because a cat's the only cat
Who knows where it's at.
I've heard some corny birds
Who tried to sing,
But still a cat's the only cat
Who knows how to swing.
Everybody wants to be a cat. Yeah!
Everybody wants to be a cat.

Later, when the music was over and the kittens were tucked into bed, Duchess and O'Malley sat out on the chimney looking over the rooftops of Paris, under a full moon. They didn't know that the kittens had climbed out of bed and were listening. O'Malley asked Duchess to stay there with him. "You know," he stammered, "the kittens need a—sort of a, kind of a—father around." "Oh, darling," said Duchess, "that would be wonderful, but we can't leave Madame. We just have to go home tomorrow."

"Well, I'm going to miss you, Baby, and those kids," O'Malley said. The listening kittens sighed, and Berlioz whispered to the others, "Gee, we almost had a father," as they tiptoed sadly back to bed.

Early the next morning, when the milk wagons were still rattling

through the streets, O'Malley and Duchess were walking toward Madame's house while the three kittens scampered on ahead. "What a fancy neighborhood! Dig these fancy wigwams!" O'Malley exclaimed. When they reached the gate, Duchess turned. "I'll never forget you, Thomas O'Malley," she said. Then she and the kittens hurried through their own little door into the house, eager to be back with their mistress, where they belonged.

Inside, Edgar was celebrating his cleverness in getting rid of the cats. With his feet on Madame's piano, drinking a bottle of Madame's best wine, he congratulated himself, "Edgar, old chap, some day this will all be yours, you sly old fox." But just at that moment he heard the meowing of kittens. "It can't be them!" Edgar exclaimed. He rushed to the kitchen and grabbed a large sack. When he saw Duchess and the kittens in the hall, he threw the sack over them before Madame could hear them. "You came back," Edgar said. "It isn't fair!" Inside the dark sack Toulouse whispered to the others, "I told you it was Edgar!"

Quickly the butler carried the bag of cats to the coach house and threw it in a trunk. "You're going to travel first class, in your own private compartment, all the way to Timbuktu!" he said as he locked the trunk. "And this time you'll never come back. The baggage truck will be here any minute to pick this up."

But Edgar hadn't counted on the cats' many friends. A little mouse called Roquefort had witnessed the entire homecoming scene. He ran off to warn the carriage horse and then caught up with O'Malley and told him what had happened to Duchess. O'Malley raced to the coach house while Roquefort went to alert the alley cat gang.

Before Edgar knew what was happening, O'Malley had jumped him and, when he got to his feet, the carriage horse kicked him down again. In no time at all the alley cats, with their leader Scat, had joined in the attack. Meanwhile Roquefort unlocked the trunk, and O'Malley tore open the sack, releasing Duchess and her kittens. Edgar lunged after them, but the alley cats and the carriage horse were too much for him. Between them they clawed and kicked the butler into the trunk, slammed the lid closed, and snapped the lock. All was ready when the baggage truck arrived.

The truck men hoisted the heavy trunk. "Heave-ho!" said one of them as they shoved it into the van. "Dis goes all de way to Timbuktu."

Madame Bonfamille was happily reunited with her beloved cats. She never knew why or how they had disappeared for a day and a night, but Duchess seemed to have found a new friend on her outing. "Duchess," said Madame, "I think this young man is very handsome. Shall we keep him in the family?" Then, as she no longer had a butler since Edgar's sudden and mysterious departure, she added, "We need a man around the house."

Madame changed her will to include O'Malley, but more than that, she set up a fund for all the homeless alley cats of Paris. From that time on, it was not only the aristocats who enjoyed the good life.

THE ARISTOCATS

The Story of the Production

Pre-production work was begun in 1963 on this feature, the twenty-third and last of the full-length animated films, starting with *Snow White,* with which Walt Disney himself was at all involved. He had seen Ken Anderson's board of drawings and approved the production plans before he died in December, 1966. But when *The Aristocats* was released in 1970, it was the first film produced in its entirety without him.

The production team was headed by two Disney veterans, Wolfgang (Woolie) Reitherman, who also directed, and Winston Hibler, who is perhaps best known for his nature films in the remarkable *True Life Adventure* series. Reitherman, speaking of his thirty-year association with Disney, said, "I think a little of Walt rubbed off on all of us. That guy was always deeply involved in his work and excited about every project. We make life happen in cartoon form." Hibler worked with Larry Clemmons and the animators on firming the story line in advance, since there would be no Walt Disney to pull everything together in the final stages of filming.

Director Woolie Reitherman runs through an amusing sequence for Vance Gerry, Eric Cleworth, Larry Clemmons, and Ken Anderson

The cast of voices was brilliant: Eva Gabor was Duchess, the fluffy white cat. About her role she said, "It's the first time I've ever done anything like this. It was complicated and difficult, dahling, because to play a cat you have to play it very human. But you have to imagine how this cat is going to react and move, so it needs a lot of thought." Phil Harris (the voice of Baloo the Bear in *The Jungle Book*) was the rough, tough alley cat hero, O'Malley. English character actress Hermione Baddeley created the voice for Madame Bonfamille, the wealthy owner and benefactor of the aristocats. Sterling Holloway spoke for Roquefort the mouse, and Scatman Crothers did the singing and swinging for Scat Cat.

The title song of this picture, set in Paris, was recorded by none other than "Mr. Paris" himself, Maurice Chevalier, who came out of retirement at eighty-two to do it out of respect for Walt Disney. He rehearsed the number once, and recorded a perfect take the first time.

This delightful animated musical comedy, budgeted at over $4 million, is considered to be among the ten best full-length Disney films.

The premiere of *The Aristocats,* at the Westwood Village theater in California, was enlivened by Disney Christmas characters

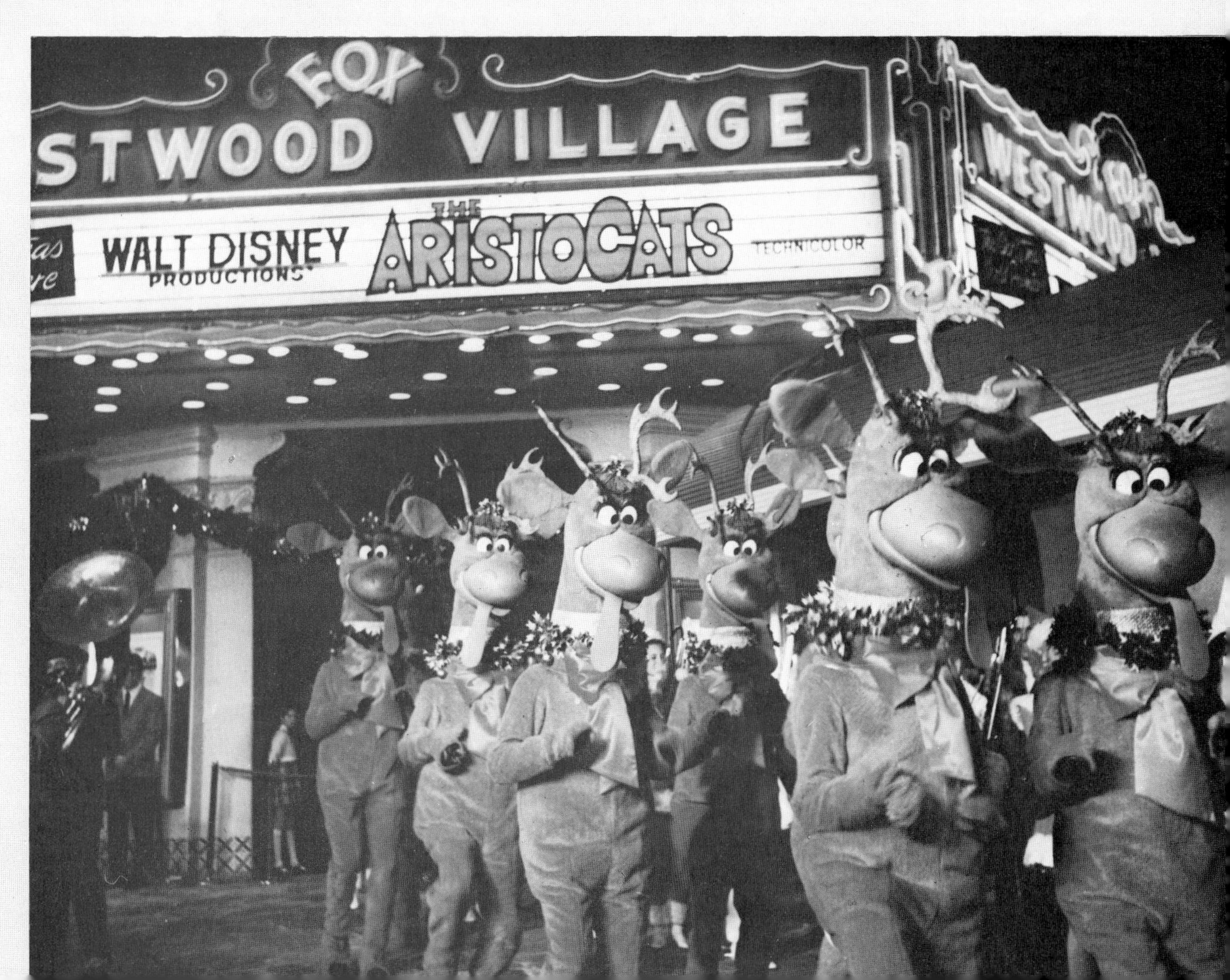
FOX
STWOOD VILLAGE
WALT DISNEY
PRODUCTIONS
THE ARISTOCATS
TECHNICOLOR
WESTWOOD

Authorized Walt Disney Productions' Edition
The Rescuers
Featuring characters from the Disney film suggested
by the books by Margery Sharp, The Rescuers and Miss Bianca,
published in the United States by Little, Brown and Company,
and in the United Kingdom by William Collins Sons and Company

RESCUE AID SOCIETY
Est. 456 B.C.

On a dark, moonless night in Devil's Bayou, a little girl clutching her teddy bear tiptoed across the deck of an old riverboat. Quickly she dropped a bottle over the side of the boat, and when she heard it splash she whispered, "Rescue me, somebody. Who will rescue me?" Then, before she could be missed, she hurried back into the boat's cabin. The bottle, with her message inside, floated from the river to the ocean, where currents carried it, many weeks later, into faraway New York Harbor.

In the United Nations Building in New York an important emergency meeting was taking place inside a steamer trunk stored in the basement. This was the headquarters of the International Rescue Aid Society, a group of mice from all over the world who helped people in trouble. They had been summoned because a bottle with a message addressed to the Morningside Orphanage had been found: I AM IN TURIBLE TRUBBLE PLEASE HURRY HELP PENNY. Seawater had washed away the rest of the message, leaving very little information to go on.

But Miss Bianca, a beautiful mouse who was one of the society's special agents, felt sorry for the little girl and was determined to help her. She asked the Chairman of the meeting if she could search for Penny, and she chose Bernard, the janitor, as her co-agent. The Chairman was surprised. "Dear lady, it's absolutely without precedent. A lady? And a jánitor? Good heavens!" "Oh, come on," Miss Bianca retorted, "we'll be a great team together." And so they were.

Bianca and Bernard's first stop was at the Morningside Orphanage, where they hoped to find some clues to the missing child. Instead they found the orphanage cat named Rufus, who was too old to chase mice and was terribly grumpy when he saw them. "If folks find out that mice moved in here I'll lose my job," he complained. When Bianca and Bernard explained that they'd leave as soon as they found out what had happened to Penny, Rufus was helpful. "Last time I saw the poor little thing she was sittin' over there on her bed all alone, lookin' awful sad because no one choosed her on Adoption Day," he told them. But Rufus didn't believe Penny had run away, because he had cheered her up and she had hugged him and said, "I love you, Rufus."

However, after further questioning by Bianca and Bernard, the cat recalled a weird-looking lady who owned a sleazy pawnshop down the

street, and who had tried to give Penny a ride in her car. "Penny wouldn't have anything to do with scum like her," he reported.

"Miss Bianca," said Bernard, "we must go down there and investigate. We gotta find her and help her."

"Yeah," said Rufus, "but two little mice—what can *you* do?"

That night the two rescuers crawled under the door of Medusa's Pawn Shop and looked around the cluttered interior. On the desk Bianca spied a child's book with a red cover, and when Bernard opened it, there was Penny's name written inside! "She's gotta be here!" Bernard exclaimed.

Just then the telephone rang loudly behind them. The two mice jumped with fright and in a flash both disappeared into a cubbyhole.

Medusa strode angrily into the room and picked up the phone. The mice heard her scolding someone called Snoops because he hadn't found the diamond yet. Then their little pink ears really pricked up when she said, "You caught Penny sending messages in bottles? Can't you even control a little girl? Shut up!" She slammed down the receiver and muttered, "I am taking the next flight down to Devil's Bayou."

While Medusa was packing, Bianca and Bernard managed to hide themselves in her suitcase. But, once they were in the car, Medusa drove like a madwoman, and the suitcase took one great bounce off the back seat and flew out onto the sidewalk, spilling clothes and combs and cosmetics—and the mice—all over, while the car sped off into the distance. Now they would have to get to Devil's Bayou some other way.

Being mice, Bianca and Bernard could not, of course, travel on commercial airlines. By great good fortune they were able to book on Albatross Airlines, a one-bird operation managed and piloted by Captain Orville. Bernard was a little nervous and would have preferred a train, but Bianca and the Captain convinced him that the flight would be safe. "Remember," said Bianca, "we will see Penny tomorrow."

Down at Devil's Bayou, Penny had decided she must escape because, now that Medusa had arrived, life was even more difficult. Carrying her teddy bear, the brave little girl walked off the riverboat and into the scary swamp jungle, hoping that she would find her way to a town. When Medusa discovered that Penny was missing she sent her two pet crocodiles, Nero and Brutus, out into the swamp with the orders, "Bring her back, boys." The great green beasts slithered into the water in pursuit of the little girl. Meanwhile Medusa's partner, Snoops, sent up rocket flares to light up the swamp, and Medusa roared off in her swampmobile to aid in the search for Penny.

Captain Orville was just coming in for his landing approach at Devil's Bayou when the rocket flares burst in the air around him. "Sufferin' Sassafras!" the Albatross exclaimed as his tail feathers caught on fire. "Bail out!" he yelled to his two passengers. Luckily, cautious Bernard never traveled without his umbrella, and the mice used it now for a parachute. Orville, after dousing his tail feathers in the swamp, flew off for repairs.

When Bianca and Bernard landed, they were befriended by two kindly swamp rats, Luke and Ellie Mae. The rats were delighted to help them. "We swamp folks," said Luke, taking a swig from his jug, "would sure like to run that Medusa clean out of our bayou." "Hold it, hold it," Ellie Mae ordered, pushing them all into the reeds. "Somebody's coming this way!"

Horrified, Bianca and Bernard peered up through the leaves at two monstrous crocodiles, one carrying a little girl in his jaws, the other carrying a teddy bear. "It's Penny!" said Bianca. "Oh, how terrible."

"She's tried to run away again," Ellie Mae explained. "They're takin' her back to the ole riverboat, Medusa's hideout."

Luke and Ellie Mae shouted for Evinrude, a dragonfly who had the fastest boat in the swamp, a large leaf that he pushed with a buzzing sound like that of an outboard motor. The mice clambered aboard, and off they zoomed to follow the crocodiles.

When they climbed out of Evinrude's little craft and reached the deck of the riverboat, Bernard called down, "Stick around, Evinrude. We'll signal if we need you." Then, just as the mice were crossing the deck, Bianca shouted, "Look out! Here she comes!" and both mice

ducked for cover. Medusa's swampmobile skidded up the gangplank, bounced on the deck a few times, then came to a screeching stop with a loud explosion of its exhaust.

Medusa stormed into the riverboat, screaming at Snoops, "Where is the little brat?" Bianca and Bernard climbed a rope and peered through the window. They heard Medusa demand, "I want her to find that big diamond, the Devil's Eye. I don't want this junk," as she knocked Snoops's handful of small diamonds to the floor with her cane. "Ouch!" cried Snoops when she struck his hand. Medusa then explained how she planned to lower Penny down the Black Hole into the pirates' cave where the fabulous diamond was hidden. "You didn't leave the child down in the cave long enough, Snoops. Tomorrow she stays down until she finds the Devil's Eye—or else!"

Bianca and Bernard realized there was no time to lose. They had to rescue Penny from this dreadful woman at once. The mice scampered along the deck until they came to the window of Penny's room. The little girl had put Teddy's nightcap on him, and she and her bear were saying their prayers. "And please let someone find my bottle," she sobbed. "There's a message in it."

Bianca and Bernard slipped through the window and onto Penny's pillow. "Penny dear," they whispered, "don't cry. We found your bottle and we're here to help you." Together they planned the escape for that very night. Bernard and Bianca would lure the crocodile guards into a cage. Perhaps Bianca's fancy French perfume could be used as bait. When Nero and Brutus were safely locked away, the rescuers and Penny would make their escape in Medusa's swampmobile. Bernard called down to Evinrude, who had been waiting nearby, and asked him to round up all the swamp folk to help—quickly.

Evinrude buzzed off on his mission, but two hungry bats chased him, their mouths open and ready to devour the little dragonfly, their jaws snapping at his tail. Just in time Evinrude spied a bottle and dived into it while the bats flapped their wings in frustration on the outside.

Before Bianca and Bernard had a chance to put their rescue plan into operation Medusa and Snoops burst into Penny's room. "Hurry and get dressed," Medusa ordered. "We're going to the pirates' cave right away to take advantage of the low tide." The mice quickly slipped into Penny's pocket where, small though they were, their secret presence was a comfort to the little girl.

At the entrance to the Black Hole Penny balked at having to be lowered into the dark and dangerous cave. Medusa snatched Penny's teddy bear. "I'll just keep him up here with me. You get down there and find that big diamond or you'll never see Teddy again!" she shouted. Unhappily, Penny climbed into the bucket and was lowered through the small opening. "Boss," said Snoops in admiration, "you've really got a way with kids."

Down in the damp, echoing cavern Penny, Bernard, and Bianca could hear the sound of the sea booming against the rock. "Way back there is the hole where the water comes in at high tide," Penny told them. "Well, if I were a pirate that's just where I'd hide the Devil's Eye," said Bernard. "I'll ah . . . I'll . . . I'll go over and check it out." While Penny held the lantern, Bernard and Bianca explored deep within

the pirates' cave. The tide was rising, and at the last possible moment the mice found the brilliant diamond embedded in the eye socket of a skull. When they pried it out it was bigger than they were!

"Medusa, I found it!" Penny called. "Hurry and pull me up!" She and the mice jumped into the bucket just as the rising water flooded into the cave. When they reached the surface, greedy Medusa snatched the diamond. She scarcely allowed Snoops to see the prize jewel, though half of it was supposed to be his and, back at her hideout, she secretly concealed the diamond in Penny's teddy bear. When Penny pleaded for the return of Teddy, Medusa laughed cruelly. "Teddy goes with me, my dear. I've grown quite fond of him."

Meanwhile Evinrude had eluded the bats and had buzzed the alarm to the swamp folk. They had joined forces and launched an attack on Medusa's boat. Now was the time for Bernard's escape plan. He and the swamp people tripped Medusa before she could reach her swampmobile. As Medusa went sprawling, the teddy bear flew out of her hands. Penny grabbed it and ran for the swampmobile, while Medusa screamed to the crocodiles, "After her, boys!" Brutus and Nero slithered off in pursuit of Penny, but Bianca and Bernard ran in front of them to divert them.

Using her mouse-sized atomizer, Bianca sprayed perfume in their path. The crocodiles skidded to a stop and sniffed the delicious air, uttering grunts of delight. Spraying perfume as she ran, Bianca led them away from Penny and right into the cage.

Penny, Bianca, and Bernard made their getaway safely while the Swamp Volunteers, an honorary branch of the International Rescue Aid Society, cheered happily.

A few days later, back in New York, Bianca and Bernard watched a television newscast that took place on the steps of the Morningside Orphanage. There was Penny with her new mother and father, who had chosen her from among all the other children in the orphanage. She was not only adopted, she was a heroine! The television reporter announced that the Devil's Eye, the world's largest diamond, had been given to the Smithsonian Institution. "Penny," he added, "you were a brave little girl to do what you did all by yourself."

"Oh," Penny replied, "I didn't do it all by myself. Two little mice, Bernard and Bianca, from the Rescue Aid Society helped me. Could I say hello to them? Hello, Bianca. Hi, Bernard."

The reporter smiled at the television audience and shook his head. "Ah," he said, "the wonderful imagination of a child!"

THE RESCUERS

The Story of the Production

The international success of this full-length cartoon feature, released in July, 1977, is a tribute to the ongoing talents of the Disney creative team forty years after *Snow White and the Seven Dwarfs.* The film was in production for four years, at a cost of more than $6 million. In six months, revenues from foreign distribution alone exceeded $21 million, a record for any Disney film.

Ron Miller was the executive producer and Wolfgang (Woolie) Reitherman produced and co-directed with John Lounsbery and Art Stevens. Between them these men put in 136 years at the Studio! But more significantly for the future, *The Rescuers* also marks the feature-length debut of a remarkable group of young animators. Working under the supervision of veterans Ollie Johnston, Milt Kahl, and Frank Thomas, whose animation has graced every Disney film since the 1930s, the new staff of twenty-five artists came up through the Studio's Talent Development Program.

The Rescuers and *Miss Bianca,* by the British author Margery Sharp, inspired the film's story about two resourceful and courageous mice who rescue a kidnapped orphan from the clutches of a villainess. According to Miss Sharp's publisher, the Disney production helped put *all* the Miss Bianca books on the bestseller list.

A stellar cast lent their voices and talents to the characters. Bob Newhart is heard on the soundtrack as mild but stalwart Bernard, the mouse janitor who embarked on a heroic mission. Eva Gabor's charm and sophistication fit that "minx of a mouse," Miss Bianca, like one of the heroine's tiny suede gloves. The crucial role of the arch-villainess, Madame Medusa, is given its melodramatic yet humorous voice by the fine dramatic actress Geraldine Page. And the weary voice of Captain Orville, the one-bird Albatross Airlines, belongs to none other than Jim Jordan, radio's "Fibber McGee."

In developing the final script, writer Larry Clemmons (who doubled in brass as the voice of Gramps, one of the swamp folks) and his staff spent a year working on rough storyboard sketches, trying to establish the characters. "It doesn't happen overnight," said Clemmons. "The voice and personality of the actors become a major influence, too. We keep making changes until we have the final story and script ready for the animators. They take the characters, situations, and words and make it all come to life."

Looking at the animation drawings of the characters they represent, the cast recording the Swamp Folks' voices throw themselves into their parts